YoungWriters

TEEN POETS

IMMERSED IN VERSE

EDITED BY SHOBHNA PATEL

First published in Great Britain in 2014 by:
YoungWriters
Remus House
Coltsfoot Drive
Peterborough
PE2 9BF
Telephone: 01733 890066
Website: www.youngwriters.co.uk

Book Design by Ashley Janson

SB ISBN 978-1-78443-038-2

Printed and bound in the UK by BookPrintingUK
Website: www.bookprintinguk.com

FOREWORD

As part of our ongoing pursuit to present a showcase of today's best up-and-coming poets, Young Writers is proud to present its 'Teen Poets' series.

Few periods in life are more turbulent or more crucial in human development than in the early teens. The struggles and trials faced daily can shape and mould our developing persona as we take a tentative step towards our early adult lives. The 'Teen Poets' series aims to bring these growing tribulations to light, providing a valuable snapshot into the thoughts and poetic visions of the teenage mind.

Immersed In Verse offers a selection of these poems, as the young writers within tackle a range of vital issues whilst also sharing with us the lighter side of teenage life. The result is a valuable and stimulating insight into the mind-set of the modern youth, and an engaging read for many years to come.

CONTENTS

THE POEMS

I REJECTED YOUR LOVE

The amount of love you had for me,
It's a shame that was something I couldn't really see.
You loved me immensely,
And I was the one that pushed you away,
But still you put me in your heart and you stayed.
Life has many, many ways,
From every corner and every side,
But today I am hurt right inside.
I regret what I did to you,
I wish I wasn't immature,
And I wish I could've given you more.
What I put you through,
I am going through that today,
And now you're with someone else happily away.
My lips are sealed but my heart is speaking out loud,
You treated me right even in front of that crowd.
You're happy today and I am very depressed,
I'm going through a lot and a lot of stress!
When you were the one who was going through that,
I wasn't there, I pushed you back!
I was mean and very, very evil,
And now my lips are left to seal.
I'm not worthy to even speak to you,
Or get you to be mine
Because you deserve the best in life in every line.
I still feel for you and do cry now and then,
I know I can never ever have you again!

Arosa Ahmed (16)

LOST IN THE STARS

A wise man once told me that love is mysterious,
Love is infuriating, love is powerful
And finally love is heart-breaking,
But at the end you always find your true love.
Even if she is on the other side of the world,
Or across the stars,
But he said as long as I look upon the bright stars that shine
Amongst the pure darkness of the sky,
There will be someone, someone who will be watching the stars
And who will be waiting for me to find her.

Until that day happens I wait,
I wait for her to make me complete,
Where true happiness lies.
I'm the sun who will be getting brighter every day,
Penetrating my light to guide her towards me.

The time has passed and my thought of love has come true.
She stands before me, a vision of light,
That stands between complete perfection and of complexion.
She is the one that can bring upon the war of Troy.
The one who will bring two kings together from the far east
And from the far west to fight for her, to the battle of death.
She is the one who made the sea split by her angelic beauty.
She is my Greek goddess, my Aphrodite
Who brings all my dreams to life.
As our bodies came close together
And the heat became much stronger.
My north and her south ignited as one
And our love was pure passion and excitement,
There was not one moment of dullness with her,
Not one second was wasted with her,
When I lay next to her at night, time stopped,
At this point all I could think of is how lucky I was
To be with someone like her.

As time went on her eyes became weary
And mine became teary,
Slowly departing from this world on to the next,
Her last words were my love, my only love

We will be together once again,
But for now look upon the stars
And I will be shining until the day you will die,
Where we will be together till the end of time.

Her last breath was unforgettable
And her presence will never be forgotten,
She lies there cold but not alone, as I give her a kiss on the forehead,
I know we will be together once again one day,
Until then goodnight my true love,
There could never be a woman as beautiful as you
That can replace your space within my heart.

Aaron Ibrahim (18)

CATCHING MEMORIES

I swerve blindly to the left,
Avoiding shadows in the low light,
Heavenly skies rustling in the wind,
As I run for my life.

Memories are running away from me,
I chase them under the stars,
I follow them where they may lead me,
Only to find they have already caused harm.

And I remember a time when I dreamed,
It was about somebody wonderful,
And that person brought me happiness,
Kind of like you do now.

Claire Beardmore (15)

UNTITLED

Hugs.
Hugs turn to kisses
Kisses turn to fun
Fun turns to feelings
Feelings turn to love
Love turns to heartbreak
Hugs?

What if?
What if you lose the thing you have been looking for?
What if it breaks your heart
What if you never get it back
What if you love what you have lost
What if I was talking about you?

A light.
They say you will find the light at the end of the tunnel
But how can you
When there is no light to be found?
But that doesn't mean you can't have a torch
A light of your own.

Just because.
Just because I smile
It doesn't mean I am happy
Just because I say something nasty
It doesn't mean that I mean it
Just because you see me on my own
Doesn't mean I don't have any friends
Just because I am not like you
Doesn't mean I am different.

Poppy Prest (13)

TWO ROADS AHEAD

The cost of the devil's trickery,
He drags you forcefully across the flaming floor.
A path lies ahead.
Tempting signs lead the way.
A life of pleasing and of ease.
But in the end, the regrets will grow.
The wide road leads to destruction.
For the life of ease will change suddenly,
Into chaos and death.

As God had promised us,
We shall gain eternal life.
But from the struggles and the taunting,
The taunting of the cold-hearted,
Filled with thorns and spikes.
However the blessings are plentiful,
For the narrow road leads to being.
The path leads the way,
To everlasting peace.
Everlasting peace with our Heavenly Father.

The choice is yours,
The choice of life and the choice of death.
The choice to ignore the blessing of the One and Only.
Or the choice to gain the unmatchable prize; a seat beside our Father.
A choice to burn in sulphur,
And the choice to taste love.
The choice to slave for Satan,
And the choice to be the children of God . . .

The choice of the Two Roads ahead.

Jaison Thomas (14)

THE WALK HOME

Feel the cool air against your warm skin,
And let the goose bumps rise
Trudging through the deep, dark night
Long gone is the light
A day of work is over now
Back to home, where the nothing lies
Surrounded by cold and waiting for the dawn
The dawn where the sorrows start and the wind howls
Where you heave out of bed with dark eyes, wishing you were anywhere
Anywhere but here
And as you walk back to your small flat
You can't help but notice
The smell of lingering rot and the nearby lamp post illuminating a pool of brightness
Flickering, steadily . . . on . . . off . . . on . . . off . . .
The black shadows seem to creep up on you, mocking and taunting
Your footsteps thud before slowing, slowing, slowing, stop
Leaves brush by your booted feet as your breath shortens and becomes heavier
You gasp, eyes widening, heart thumping, worlds crashing
Because in front of you is something so unseen
So rare, and disgusting, and bloody
That no person should have to see it
A stained knife, a heap of clothes, a pale object
A dead body.

Eva Marcelle Rutherford (14)

?

Life is so unfair that complaining about it seems unfair
Un-progressing as if I'm stuck on the bottom layer
Hungry for progress as much as a bald head desires a set of hair
There's no time to take some time off and grab a little air
Work upon work, that's the content that makes up the earth's layers
In the city of political entertainment, Boris Johnson is the mayor
His work is crucially important, yet he makes it seem like he's running the
city fair

I'm out here trying to make a difference
But all I see is obstacles obstructing the path to difference
Optimism and faith can pluck the attitude of hindrance
It feels like Halloween every day because everyone has the mask of
pretence
Its purpose; to obstruct difference and be relentless in the act
I'm privileged and thankful to be where I am
It hasn't been in my doing and that's why I am glad

I must now be independent and take a leap
My experiences and visions grace me with a lead
My desired achievements unrealistic as so to be featured in my daydreams
My sanity questioned and my existence reviewed
I guess the biggest obstacle is yourself
No difference can be made without the consent of yourself
But to me, nothing makes sense.

Nash Mwangi (16)

MEMORIES

The summer flowers have withered
But I still see them grow
As bright as diamonds
Sparkling like flakes of snow.

Now I'm in December
I still remember
How they grew
Those summer flowers so blue.

They don't seem to fade away
Just like my memories
They shine every day
But they remain as stories.

I write them in my head
Just before I go to bed
I read them in my dreams
Better than hearing reality screams.

Yes, the lilies have withered
But their memory still prevails
It's just a phase
I can't seem to forget these days.

Hanan Sultan (16)

GAME OF LOVE

I don't know why, loneliness has come,
To meet me again.
At what turn has love brought me.

Is my fight against myself,
Or against God Himself,
At what turn has love brought me.

Love is a game of cards,
Of breaking and building trust.

Don't know why I think,
That I am an empty road.
Have you lost me somewhere,
Or have I gone lost myself?
Come find me again.
What should I promise you again.

I'm a broken musical instrument,
I'm angry with myself,
I'm that voice which is hidden
Somewhere in the chest.

Listen to me without saying anything.
How long can the heart bear silence.
Love is a game of cards,
Of breaking and building trust.

Aisha Shoro (15)

INIMITABLE STAR

The waves fold themselves brightly in and out,
Repeatedly.
Never stopping;
Never wanting to stop.
The moon engulfs me in its glistening rays.
Faint chanting can be heard in the distance –
They are the ever-longing calls to the one that has gone,
To remind them that they are missed.
They are loved.
They will not be forgotten.
Thousands of people stand like candles,
Weeping and wailing.
The candle of your life continues to flicker,
'The Lord is my shepherd,
I shall not want,
He makes me to lie in green pastures . . .'
The flame begins to burn even brighter.
This candle was lit in remembrance of you.
Wax drips encaustic tears,
Mourning for you as we are.
We come together for prayer.
I pray that in the dark, I can touch a star by sight.
I pray you are that star;
That its light will continue to shine
And that it will never fade away,
Because this star is brightest amongst the others.

RIP: Deacon Tekle Giorgis Akalu.

Aster Gordon (16)

EXAMS

You get up and you get dressed,
You eat your breakfast, you've had no rest,
You go to class, you look and listen,
You sit still, your muscles stiffen.
'Take notes!' they say, and, 'Will you sit down?'
But your friends are there to say, 'Don't frown!
Things get better, so don't you worry,
It's not like you're the teacher's quarry!'
You cheer up. Your friends are the best.
They always know when you're feeling stressed.
You have exams, and all you hear
Is, 'Be sure to get good grades this year!'
Is that really how it is these days?
Your future relies on your essays
And ISAs, facts, those hard questions
But when will we be in the situation
Where a Shakespearean quote will save the day
Or keep impending bills at bay?
You must still revise
And you must try hard
But when that flimsy bit of card
With those little letters – a pass or fail –
Are something of a force ten gale,
It's not the end.
There's always hope.
It doesn't matter what you wrote.
All that matters is that you stay true
To all those things that make you 'you'.

Laura Bartlett (14)

A WOMAN'S PLIGHT

Many passers stop and stare
At the people standing over there,
Just because they may look weird
Or just because they have so much fear.

No one knows the people's story
Or if they get a piece of glory,
Despite the things life throws out
They're never ones to scream or shout.

A man and a woman seems so normal
But she's anything but formal,
Forced to do some dirty favours
Just to pay off her husband's wagers.

Life for her isn't a treat
Especially when she's getting beat,
All she wants to do is hide
Until the sun comes out to shine.

But the sun won't shine until it's sorted
So let's fix up and not be distorted,
Let's raise awareness you and me
And help everyone else to see.

You never know how it can help
But she didn't have to self help,
Now she can be who she wants
Even become a debutante.

Just a little piece of advice
Girls you should never pay the price,
Of anyone's or man's mistakes
You should just be making them quake.

Mollie Woodhouse (14)

WHAT IS WAR TO YOU?

War affects us all
The conflicts and the brawl.
As long as injustice reigns
People will die in pain.

For me war is suffering,
Pain, loss, hard work and dying.
Many friends have I seen fall
And many from injury crawl.

For me war is friendship,
Ploughing together through hardship.
Friends stay close and committed
United we fight undefeated.

For me war is sadness,
The discomfort all through this madness.
Wait for news of a loved one,
We walk into reckless abandon.

For me war is family,
With a need of someone to be manly.
Through tears we will stand
And hold one another's hand.

For us war is final
All the world waits for the trial.
Together we'll fight:
For freedom – our right.

War affects us all
The conflicts and the brawl.
As long as injustice reigns
People will die in pain.

Hannah Cawthorn

WHY DO YOU HATE THE JESTER?

Why do you hate the jester?
He is the best in town
He paints smiles across their faces
smothers every frown.

Why do you hate the jester?
He has so much love inside,
with all his care and goodness,
in him one can confide.

Why do you hate the jester?
He could not dream to hurt.
His heart is soft and tender
words never cruel nor curt.

Why do you hate the jester?
I thought I knew him well
he was always by my side
but he would never tell.

Why do you hate the jester?
The colour of the court,
I did not know you before
he hid you easily, you never fought.

Why do you hate the jester?
You bring me so much pain
but it is he I weep for
with guilt I can't contain.

Why do you hate the jester?
Now it seems to all make sense,
I beg, hurt me instead,
let him drop pretence.

Why do you hate the jester?
Why do you feel alone?
Why couldn't I see behind the mask,
help you, bring you home.

Why do you hate the jester?
Jester, I do not jest,
you are beautiful. Love yourself,

as you are really loved by all the rest.

Don't mask your pain,
behind your smiles,
you are not alone.
Let others tell the jokes,
let them cease your groan

for, the jester must see,
the laughs and the highs
are not worth the fall
when I discover you,
beneath his cloak.

You don't have to be the jester
cast away the mask
share with me
drop the blade
and restart.

Kelly Norways (16)

THE MONOTONY OF UNIFORMITY

The love I experience is immense,
Yet I am obliged within to conceal.
I plea you carry on at my expense,
But my anguish endures not to reveal.
But if this is what I have to endure,
With cessation of all the mean torment,
Then I will have to hate the love allure,
Despite being a cloud of discontent.

To be normal is not to be normal;
All I wish for is to love and be loved,
Of which, how can I be an abnormal?
Yet I continue to be harshly shoved.
Difference should be the widely embraced;
Love, in any form, is not a disgrace.

Jake Symington (15)

IMAGINE

We all have a special place,
Somewhere to go,
When we dread a face,
Somewhere to sit,
Somewhere to be,
Somewhere where a coin is worth as much as a pea,
But we all know that this place can't always be,
What would be Heaven without Hell?
Life without death,
The place you go can't always be,
But that doesn't mean it can't be reality . . .

The place you go,
The place you be,
The place where you sit on trees,
Every day you go,
Every day you know,
For reality is but a word,
Fact but a thing,
But this place you be,
This is far from reality.
For every day you go,
Something new is beneath your throne . . .

The people you see,
The people you meet,
All worthless,
You know,
But who will agree,
For the place you go,
In the place you be,
Is nothing,
But a cup of tea,
But who will agree?

The place you go,
In the place you be,
Is always there,
Even after you count to three,
For this place you go,

Where you will forever be,
Is imagination,
Like a holy tree,
Where no one disagrees,
And a day,
Is a count to three.

So go to the place,
Where you will always be,
Even till the edge of eternity,
For this special place,
Where you will always be,
Is always there,
Just count to three,
It is part of you,
A piece of you,
And it will always be,
So go there now,
Go to your special place.
Imagine . . .

Patrick Hayes (13)

BIRDS

Birds, flying in the heavens
Gliding, swooping, floating
Fishes of the sky
Swimming through open air

Their flapping wings are like gills to a fish
Lungs to a human, their very survival
With every flap and swoop they mock us with their freedom
Proudly.

Our envy causes us to imitate them
Planes, air gliders, parachutes
But we are not made like them
For then would we truly appreciate freedom in nature?

Anita Idigbo (18)

BABY BEAR'S POV

I woke up in the morning to a smell so tantalising
I raced down the stairs to see a sight so appetising
Freshly-cooked bowls of porridge, one, two, three
One for Daddy;
One for Mummy;
And one for me!

Alas, the porridge was piping-hot
As it had been poured straight from the pot
Daddy reached out to pick up a bowl
But Mummy suggested we go for a stroll
So we set off for a walk in the crisp morning breeze
Holding both their hands I ran off into the trees!

Although I picked blackberries off a bramble
I was still hungry after the ramble
So, you can imagine my anticipation –
When Mummy opened the door – to eat the creation!
Eagerly waiting to scoff my meal
Suddenly Daddy gave out a squeal,
'Mummy, Baby!
The porridge is gone!'

Distress temporarily outweighing my greed
(For this was a terrible situation, indeed)
I stared hopelessly down at the bowl, when Mummy Bear
Cried out loud, 'Daddy, Baby! Where is the chair!'

Now, being kind, I possibly wouldn't have minded
As much if it wasn't my chair; but I must be reminded
That it very much was my chair!
So through my complete despair
I wondered why and how someone could do this to us;
Why would you want to kick up all this fuss?

So we were all angry, us three bears
When suddenly I heard a sound from upstairs!
Sobbing and crying, unable to speak
As I thought that my future was utterly bleak
I pointed towards the staircase
And we all clambered up them to see a peaceful face!

Sleeping so peacefully (upon my bed)
You couldn't think she was evil; but that she's innocent instead
Try as I might, I couldn't keep it in:
'Daddy, Mummy,
This bear has skin!'

As we crowded round her she awoke with a start
The skinless bear's eyes looked frightened – they started to dart
Though her mouth opened she couldn't speak
However she did manage to 'squeak'!
Daddy, on the other hand, gave a roar
And the little girl shrieked and ran out the door!

After that we never saw the strange bear again
But thankfully I got my porridge in the end!

Emily Wootton (15)

NO CHANGE

Many say they want changes
They want changes during their lifetime
They want changes for future generations

Change requires determination
It requires strength and time

Many claim they've tried to change
They claim they've tried to prevent unjust
They claim they've spoken out

Many pray for change
Wish for change
Search for change

Many want change, but will not change
They wait for change.

Khadijah Abdullahi (14)

DRUGS

I smoke weed every day 'cause I'm under stress,
It's a regret I say but some days I need it,
Whatever you think I don't give a ****,
I bet you lot are whispering to each other: *OMG,*
She's mad taking all these drugs.
But deep inside she wants to cry.

Chelsea Marie Jordan

THE OPPOSITE OF TEA

The price of coffee
So much more than toffee
Rich Columbian drink
Stimulates my mind to make me think

If the price so high, £2.99
Why do I feel like I fly
Every time I buy
I get slightly high

Coffee is very addictive
But not so that it's restrictive
Wake up every morning
If there is no coffee I will need a warning

But when the day ends
The coffee has to blend
With the silky smooth cream
That helps my self-esteem.

Matthew Connon

NATURE AND THE WORLD AROUND US

The world around us is shrinking because of pollution
And our nature is suffering.
We keep on building on every bit of land we can get
But we do not think about the nature
Or the animals that live in the habitats we destroy.
They all have feelings too but nobody seems to care
But those who are working at it to try and save it in the long run
But others do not care,
We seem to think that we humans are superior to the animals
And that we can do what we want to their lives and homes
But I have just one question to ask,
How would you feel if your home and life was destroyed?

Emily Curtis (14)

UNTITLED

May all your endless days and sleepless nights be blessed with the presence of an angel watching over you and making all your days worthwhile.

May all your closest friends and furthest family be loved and cared for by you and those you love and cherish the most.

May the heavens shine on you, pull you out of your bad times, hold you by the hand and guide you through your future.

May all that you have earned and all that you will receive from life stay by your side until it is time for you to let it go.

May you take whatever comes your way and let it help you become a better person and build a greater relationship between you and God.

Shania (14)

FOR YOU

For you a seed was planted
Deep down in my core
I watered and watched it
And prized it for sure.

It gave me hope
And played its role,
Pumped love through my veins
And fed delight to my soul.

I wanted to show you
But didn't even make a sound.
But the day I did
I had to burn it to the ground.

I proclaimed my love
But you made me hurt.
You pointed out my flaws
And compared me to dirt.

I will never forget
The day you chose her
You broke my heart
Good day to you sir.

Heidenara Carvalho (15)

MY NIECE

(Dedicated to Zoya)

The scent within odour,
The softness of a stinging bee,
The sweetness in bitter chocolate,
The beauty of a rose above thorns.

The sunshine after gloomy clouds,
The breeze of a hot day,
The rainbow after darkness,
The shade in the sizzling sun.

The shininess in hard metal,
The detail in the night sky,
The brightness of the moon,
The colours in life.

The happiness in sadness!
The crown of the family,
The princess of our lives,
The love of my life,
My niece . . .

Noor Khan (15)

THROUGH THE EYES OF A CHILD

Children have it all figured out
Smiles that will make your heart melt
And yet adults claim
That they know the way
To deal with the problems life's dealt

A child is blissfully happy
Not rude, violent nor snappy
And yet adults are seen
As a knowledge machine
And know what our life should be

Children can laugh away the day
No bigger problems than what to play
And yet adults still stress
That they know best
But worry with debts to pay

Life would be oh so pleasant
If everyone was like a child. Innocent
No racism or pain
No greed or selfish gain
If we lived in our past not present

A child can sit and watch the world go by
Joy can make their hearts fly
If only adults could make their hearts more mild
And see the world through the eyes of a child.

Becky Trimm (16)

BEING A TEEN

I've only been a teen for a month but it's been great,
being treated with respect and not like a little kid anymore.

It's been a whale of a time some days and I have had some tough ones,
but when me and my best friend resolved our argument,
it meant too much to me. I cried.

My feelings are a roller coaster and not always fun
and all my friends help me through it all
and make me seem like I'm the happiest girl in the world.

In a roller coaster you can feel angry as well as upset,
like when another girl comes up to you and starts talking
and you hate them so much and you just feel angry
when they follow you because they need to grow up big time.

Also when you fall out with your parents and siblings it's the worst,
I've got to say it's quite upsetting when you're really angry at them
and you just want to sit in a corner and cry.

I always think sometimes that everyone just needs a very good cry.
But also that they need a good laugh and a smile.

My mam tells me everyone has different feelings
and that everyone's on a different roller coaster,
some are more scary and upsetting than the one you are on.

Amie Niamh Ridley (13)

KEEP SMILING

You're alone in a place where nobody can see you.
No one to talk to, nowhere to run.
Tired and stressed to a point you give in.
Not bothered about anything, can't describe the pain within.

Angry and frustrated you shout at them all.
You eventually talk, but it's like talking to a brick wall.
People try but it just doesn't work,
So you tell them to go and leave you alone.

They think you're attention seeking, but they just don't know.
Know how it feels to be like this, to wonder why the pain won't stop!

Life is a roller coaster, full of surprises
But sometimes this pain just rises and rises.
You break down and cry, shouting, 'Why, why, why?'

Then one day you see the light, it's time to leave the bad times behind.
Enjoy your life, forgive and be kind.

You're not alone, people can see you,
Now think of the good times that you want to hold on to.

Keep smiling and laughing because they just can't.
Can't ever put you down as you're the wise one
And your invincibility has already begun.

Keep smiling and laughing, remember you're unique.
Keep smiling and laughing, my little loved one.

Georgia-Leigh Hall (13)

LET OUR FINGERS DANCE

Thus our fingers dance as our lips quiver to
Each heartbeat through the darkening night.
Only to find out that the night is spent and
The birds chatter from their luscious branches.
Yet our fingers still dance to each other's
Soulful symphonies.

The sunlight dims giving birth to a scarlet furnace
Twirling above the heavens.
Thus our love can still be heard through the drumming
Of one's fingertips entwined with our fluttering hearts;
That can be heard as gentle flapping of a
Hummingbird's wing.

Even as our eyes fall heavy, our minds do not tire.
Nor do our dancing fingers that control the night.
The moon arises from its slumber, giving heed
To the timid sapphires and gems alike.
We are so far away, though our smiles shine
So close.

We shall talk from day to night, dawn to dusk,
Sunrise to sunset.
As the ink blanket surrounds us in
An alcove of darkness.
To when the clouds hang high above,
Guarding the horizon
Talk until the birth of dawn, a new day, a new beginning.

Joshua Ford (16)

ALIVE?

I am waiting for the blur of motion.
Waiting
Waiting
And then I am blinded by the reality
Which faces me.
The world rushes by in its beautiful chaos
And I feel alive.

I want to stay this way,
Flying freely,
So I'll choose escape;
The track above and below me
Elongates each time I try to jump.
I am strapped into the choking harness
Of this life, which relaxes and I believe
That I am free now.

Yet my feet touch the ground again
And the world continues around me.
I walk off this roller coaster and onto the next,
As adrenaline claims me once more;
Stealing me for meagre seconds before I am plunged,
Back into reality, hurtling downwards,
As I realise that I had thought I had made progress,
When I had just repeated the loop, again.

Allegra Goodwin (15)

THE BOX

This is the box they made for me,
Where I will lie for centuries,
Decaying slowly underneath,
Never again to wake from sleep.
Will they not visit my body?
When I am cold and jealousy's
Taken over what's left of me.

This is the box they made for me,
Red roses and a cypress tree,
Withered and ripe with misery.
Age has stolen my vanity.
Buried with my bones and my grief,
I ring the bell desperately.
The sodden earth consumes my screams.

This is the box they made for me,
Where angels weep in purgatory.
I'll never dream, I'll never breathe.
Remember how I used to be.
How I hate this box and its greed,
When it swallows the best of me.
I'm scared to death of the lonely.

Florence Chilver (15)

ALWAYS

Standing at the window
Opening it afar
With everything that makes you wonder
Just who you are

Leaning out
Feeling that autumn breeze
It comes towards you hitting your cheeks

Blowing strands of hair
Here, there and everywhere
Itching your face
Itching your neck
Itching everywhere may not have realised
That you have left

What can you hear?
The screams of the blow
As it hits the window
And bounces off following the flow

The tree in the distance it blows not a lot
But the leaves rustle exaggerating that plot
They rustle as they fall
It's their last dying screams
But there's no different
Dying just like you and me

That old rusty swing
Swaying with the music of god
Creaking and cracking
As it has aged quite a lot

There's a cover that blows revealing what's inside
Mysteriously like two criminals trying to hide
What they are dealing to each other
Not for other's eyes
Just for one another
Secrets can be revealed
If you look and wonder why
Don't be oblivious

To what you feel inside

Look up now at what some says the sky
But maybe it's another sea just way up high
It's tarnished with white
Smothered with highlights
That drifted from afar
But will leave before the night's over by far

Up there are some lights
Many of them shine
Some say they're dreams that we try to hide
But maybe they are the doorways to Heaven
That are held open for us
Till our time is given
They are so many miles away
But we can still see them
They are present today
One day they will go
Just fade away
So enjoy them right now
The way they are today

Beauty can come from anything
Even the backyard
The closer you look
The clearer you see
Follow this and you will go far

You may think you are alone here tonight
But don't be fooled
Just because you are the only one here that's alive
I am here with you
So don't turn out that light
I will hold open your door
Until the time is right
I'm by your side
Always
Not just tonight.

Amelia Nemeth (15)

GENDER PROBLEM FOR A TEEN

Growing up a little boy confused,
Why do I have to wear this dress?
Why do I have to like the colour pink?
And why can't I play catch with Dad like my little brother does?

I don't understand the skin I am in,
Biting my fingers down to their bone,
To see if their bones were the same colour as their strips,
Finding out I am an alien bleeding the most unknown colour
Of the rainbow, why can't I be yellow, purple or blue
Instead of being beaten down to the combinations of blue and black?
It's a thing, my gender pronouns are *he* and *him*,
I use them in the same preferred sentences
But it seems no respect, they only neglect them
And continue to call me by the characteristics of my body.
My gender is male.
I never really got called a girl or a boy
Because the struggle would be less real if I looked like your nephew,
Your son, your homie, why can't I be like your husband?

Strong arms full of testosterone shaping the body into one
I will never be in
Growing to a height I will never reach in
Holding onto a child never made by my seed, I plead
God tell me why you gave me the body of Eve but the mind from Adam?
They say Eve was made from Adam so is that why I am missing
Something from the left of my side? I cried.
Does my gender affect who I am?

Cinthia Jefia (15)

LIGHTS IN THE DARKNESS

Lights in the darkness
Guiding roamers to their land
Lights in the darkness
Reaching out its calloused hand

Lights in the darkness
Illuminating the night sky
Lights in the darkness
Like the Grim Reaper's scythe

Lights in the darkness
Showing us the way
Lights in the darkness
Keeping shadows at bay

Lights in the darkness
Yet casts shadows of their own
Lights in the darkness
Luring us to wander alone

Lights in the darkness
Could be a curse or a star
Lights in the darkness
Either up close or from afar

Lights in the darkness
Heed my warning carefully
Lights in the darkness
Not all of them are friendly.

Abby Walker (13)

UNTITLED

Drip, drip, drip comes from the tap
Though it does not bother the dark, black cat
Branches bashing against the windowpane
Light shining from down the lane
The noise coming from the attic
It's enough to make the hair go static
The graveyard has cold headstones in a line
It sends a shiver up my spine.

Anna Brown (14)

MARE MISCHIEF

I feel the breeze in my hair,
as I gallop on my mare.
Across the forest and heathland,
and over the vast golden sand.

She neighs in delight,
at the beautiful sight,
picks up the pace,
and my heart starts to race.

Where are we going?
There's no way of knowing.
For my mare is free to run,
until the setting of the sun.

I feel alive,
and the land does thrive.
Galloping, galloping further and beyond,
for my mare I am dearly fond.
But suddenly I'm flying through the air,
and my mare galloped off without a care.

Arabella Drake (15)

TEENAGERS

Bright coloured braces
And spots upon faces

With eyes on their phones
All walking like clones

Partying until morn'
On drugs that are the norm

Parents going crazy
With kids that are lazy

Couples get together
Fests whatever the weather

Sex in public places
Police take up chases

Fan girls write letters
There's underage betters

Disruptive behaviour
We all need a saviour

From these eight dreadful years
That all end in tears

But soon they'll be done
When the battle is won

But there will always be more
To join in the war

Against parents and teachers alike
Who should all join the strike

Against teenagers until they have passed through these years
And they give you a whole new pack of fears.

Alice Ollerhead

TIGER

The tiger prowled in the grass
The footsteps of its prey like shattering glass
The tiger pounced upon its prey
So that she shall survive another day.

Then one day the poachers came
With their evil, hellish, murdering game
They murdered her sons
With their red hot-fire spitting guns.

Her home was burnt
The hunters never learnt
That one day she won't be here
Every second this day grows more near
This very thought fills us with utter hate
Yet still now it's her head upon the plate.

Callum Herbert (13)

SLUGS

I hate slugs
I despise the way they smear my path with their repulsive stain
Slithering, sliding and skulking, it is sickening
The conquest of my garden begins

The hateful little deformed soldiers oozing with their freakish mucus
Like a snail's evil twin
A destructive devilish and deformed, grotesque monster
A hateful little slime blob
I hate slugs.

Caleb Hermit (13)

CHANGE

The handprints have disappeared,
Nothing left of them,
But I know I'm growing up fast,
My crayons and colouring books have gone,
No more colours on the walls,
But I know I'm growing up fast,
My princess make up and jewellery have gone,
A long, long time ago,
But I know I'm growing up fast,
I can't help but wish,
To have those days when I didn't have to worry,
I know I'm growing up fast,
But change is good,
Change is different,
Change is great for you and me!

Rebecca Williamson (13)

I'M JUST A TEENAGER!

I want to break free!
Make my own decisions; I don't want to be a kid,
Although I'm just a teenager what would I know?
Ageing every day but, 'Does it get easier?' we say.
Make-up, boys, drama, rumours and lies.
Full of fears of being judged and insecurity creeping up.
Who are we to say it's tough?
Exams, loss of friends, arguments and rumours.
We're just trying to find ourselves in this mixed up universe.
We are misunderstood, misinterpreted people in society today.
We have neither problems, drama or worries, apparently.
We should be happy, carefree! Why would this be?
I'm just a teenager, please set me free!

Simone Parke (14)

WHY?

Why join the army if soldiers are dying?
Why join the army if mothers are crying?
What's the point of being afraid
When you're not even getting paid?

To look into the half-known lands,
Of sharp as knife brambles and shivering hands.
Why witness this poignant feeling of ghosts and eyes,
When on the battlefield their body lies.

They were once laughing and cheerful
But died from being too fearful.
Would you really want to go through this?
Racing car bullets, deafening bombs, confused brains
And more to the list.

The soldiers thought they were being patriotic and helping
But instead they were all yelping.
All their melancholy tears were streaming like a river
And family at home were a constant shiver.
They didn't know what they got into
Do you really want to be in their shoes?
Innocent lives were taken back then,
Let's not let that happen again?

Isobel Mills (13)

SUMMER

The sun is shining
Everyone's happy
School's been a bummer
Finally, it's summer.

A break from studying
No longer stressed
Our minds will be happy
Relieved and blessed.

How to spend our summer?
That's not hard
There are so many things to do.

No more teachers
No more classes
Now I can take off my glasses
No best friends
No more friends!
Whiff . . . where the sad part begins.

My heart runs before me
As I run out the school gate
Excited to escape
To the beach, sun and endless fun
The hummer summer has begun.

Hanan Al Ojaili (16)

EULOGY FOR MY FIRST LOVE

I was stranded and marooned,
My adoration seemed pathetic.
I fell for your eternal sweetness,
Been since an in-love diabetic.

Your crescent breasts should be abolished,
Your soulful gazes should be exiled.
Make your lips and teeth illegal,
To end siege when you smiled.

If I could build a law to silence,
Your Richter-scale exciting laugh.
That vibrates in all my brain cells,
I'd refuse to let it pass.

If I could have just one more minute,
To take in every pore –
On your face, your skin, your body,
Before you fall to earthy floor.

Would have thanked to see emotion,
To be shown before I'd left.
I won't beg for salted tear,
Just a girl somewhat bereft.

I wished that you were empty,
Yet un-sad and un-alone.
All I needed was the knowledge,
That in you – good times – I'd sown.

I'm sure you laughed and cringed and gossiped,
About this boy you left behind.
You reflect in foolish idylls,
And claim rebelling made you blind.

I forgive the undermining,
Dismiss with your perfect hands –
That our love was but a kink,
In the cable of your plans.

But inside there is an echo,
There's a dripping from the tap.
You yearn for truth and not deceit,

Again I am the 'X' on your map.

And during all my office years,
Of white-swept walls and smoking breaks.
Of birthday cakes with '3's on them,
Portfolios of mistakes.

I would stare and sit and wonder,
Did it occupy you too?
If for all our childish play,
I helped create the 'forever' you.

If in one world it would seem,
An ink spot on the page of life –
Could bring us face to face,
Pen to paper, bread to knife.

You made ripples in the puddle,
In youth, I mistook for an ocean.
Can you falsify the injustice,
Of my heart's aching – still devotion?

Whoever and where ever,
And whatever you've become –
You'll remain an old framed picture,
Of my perfect girl so young.

Now as you stared into the darkness,
You wait for garden, wait for light.
Please devastate my heart again.
Kiss me. Make me alright.

This world is good, this world is flawed,
But once I saw you and felt complete.
I'm champion of love's competition,
For you forced me to compete.

Poppy Doran (17)

HIDDEN

You're in a room full of people
All dressed in black
All but one
You; the one who stands out

The one dressed in colour
Not afraid to shine
To show who you are
And not be shy

No one understands
Though they try
But they can't
Unless they're on the inside

Day in, day out
We support the ones we love
With little support ourselves
'Cause no one understands

There's no need to hide
You should be proud
You're strong
Don't let others put you down

Ignore all those bullies
They just don't understand
They're just trying to hurt you
It's what they do best

You're stronger than an army
Just believe in you
You're a young carer
So be honoured and stand proud.

Tasha Cuthbert (15)

THOUGHTS OF YOU

Curiosity ponders the mind,
With troubled and calloused thoughts,
As to whether or not you notice I'm not in your life.

Or whether or not you miss me,
Like the sun misses the rain and the clouds miss the sky,
My heart burns like the fiery flames that get put out by the surrounding sea.

Beneath the sea lies the core,
A core bearing a still beating heart protected by this hardened shell,
To get to the inside you have to crawl into the tiny hole and through the tiny door.

The tiny door shows you the way,
The way to how I feel and how you leave me with nothing but happiness,
Happiness surrounded by anger and hatred and when you leave all I feel is shame.

Shamed by the fact you won,
I gave up trying with nothing but bitterness and negative emotion left,
If I pushed on through maybe we would have made the perfect couple together as one.

As I sit there in a puddle of melancholy,
I question whether some of my advances had been in fact misconstrued,
Misinterpreted as what you would call friendly jokes but to me us together being jolly.

There are no other ways to show you,
To show you thoughts and feelings by waving huge banners in your face,
Loving cards sent to your doorstep with relations to your favourite things that make your smile shine through.

All you do is inspire my success,
Occasionally bumping into you at work makes me smile for the rest of the day,
I want us to happen to show you that I just want to try and match your perfectness.

Simon Brooks

MY TEENAGE YEARS

It felt like yesterday that I was a baby crawling about the house
I woke up this morning a teenager at last
Being a teenager is awesome you can do so many things,
Go shopping, swimming, or even work in KFC
Even though being a teenager is great it also comes with a price
It's painful, emotional, Mother Nature's not nice
Sometimes you don't know what you're doing, it sneaks up on you like a ghost
You take your anger and hate out on the ones you love the most
Yes, you have more freedom than when you were a little kid;
You are adventurous, skilful with so many things
Your body is important in this time, keep fit and healthy all the while
I know this because I'm now a teenager myself, I go through the emotions like anyone else
I enjoy being a teenager I really do, it's scary at times but I pull through
Now I leave you this message to help you through
The tough time that is in front of you
Live life to the full and never look back, you are who you are
And never change that.

Rayanne Creer (13)

ADOLESCENCE

He's got ruffled hair and loose jeans,
I think he's finding his way in the world.
She's got make-up on her face to try to impress,
I guess that's adolescence at its best.

She doesn't care about the day.
There's other things on her mind, let's just say.
He doesn't know what he's worth.
Staying strong is painful for him sometimes.

The glass bottle beneath the sandwiches,
Doesn't describe all of us.
The cry for help in a quiet head is hard to hear,
This describes most of us.

We're the same, just a bit different.
We're unique.
We try to impress,
That's just adolescence at its best.

We want to live life.
We wish to forget and move on.
Everyone only lives once.
We're in the phase called adolescence.

Gabrielle McMaster (15)

HAPPINESS

Happiness always comes with a cost
Either a loved one dies
Either a relationship fails
Either having an argument with a loved one.
Happiness is something that you cannot force or buy.
But you have to earn.
Life offers many chances to learn from your mistakes
Or having to deal with a lost one.
We never get the chance to be happy at our fullest
Happiness is precious like gold
So when you get it keep it safe and bold
Sometimes when feeling down.
You just need something that makes you happy
Favourite actor or actress
Or your pets
Or your family or friend
Or
By just reading a book
A smile doesn't last for long
So when you do
Keep it as long as you can.

Virgina Tharmapalan (17)

MY POEM

We once met in Year 7 that's where it really began,
No one knew what lay ahead, let's say a mystery,
Getting lost around school not knowing where to go,
Scared of taller pupils towering down upon you,
Slowly becoming used to it you gain confidence
Meet new friends, teachers, and people.

Year 8 our minds started to develop and adapt to
This new lifestyle, you grow taller and suddenly towering
Pupils don't become so scary and you start to outgrow them
Our form class one big family like no other form class
Relationships between boys and girls start to become a regular thing
Boys' friendship becomes stronger and girls continue to fight and make up.

Year 9 where we start to become young adults top of the lower school
At the start you wonder where the last two years have gone
You start to worry about where you are, are you cool?
Appearance becomes an issue, girls' make-up and boys' hair
Heads of year complain about make-up and hair products
Pupils think it's not fair
Coming towards the end of Year 9 and once again you start to think
'The big years are coming'.

Ryan Goburdhone (14)

ANGER MANAGEMENT

A burning fire that will always be there internally,
Remaining dormant until the right time comes waiting,
Like a volcano I'm ready to erupt like never before,
Why do I feel like this?

A violent army ready for war to break out immediately,
Guns at the ready with the soldiers in formation waiting,
Finger on the trigger ready to draw blood,
Why do I feel like this?

A vicious cheetah hunting for its dinner stalking,
Blending in with the surroundings waiting,
Claws out ready for the inevitable time to pounce,
Why do I feel like this?

Breathe in . . .
. . . Breathe out,
Count to ten,
Remain calm.

Sam Bailey (16)

CHAINS

Daddy, Daddy please listen to me cry,
It is not my wish that I soon may die,
Don't blame Mum either. She is too weak,
I know water is thin, and blood is thick.
Daddy, Daddy please listen to me cry.

Daddy, Daddy please don't let me go.
I'm your child and dear; let him know.
Fight for me, Daddy. Please let me live,
Take away my chains; my life is not to give.
Daddy, Daddy please don't let me go.

Daddy, you have let me go now,
Traded my heart before the crowd.
Traded my life for a dented pocket,
Freedom, under this roof, I will never get.

Mummy, please tell Daddy to look at my scars,
Ask Daddy to lift me up to reach the distant stars,
I know you would. I know you could.

But I know you won't.

Phoebe Ruguru (16)

HALLOWEEN

On this night of Halloween,
The dead arise for Witch McEean.
'Come now, come now, let's all go.'
So the dead lurched out of the eerie glow.

This is what happens when the dead are seen,
As such is the terror of Halloween.
Bats, pumpkins and things that rot
The dead devised a fiendish plot.
'Come my pretties,' screeched Witch McEean,
'Let's kill them all, we'll wipe them clean.'

A deathly voice came out of the gloom,
'There's too much light, it's nearly full moon.
The werewolves are out and you know I hate dogs,
Besides all that we were sleeping like logs.'
The others joined in on a similar tone,
'It's too warm out here, it gets down to the bone.'

'Oh you pathetic bunch, if it's not blood you crave
Then you might as well go back to the grave.'
So the dead returned to their lairs unseen
And the living stayed safe till next Halloween.

Kirti Holmes-Brown (14)

BETRAYAL POEM

Sitting here,
alone once more.
Slowly the tears begin to fall,
as I gaze, transfixed,
knowing she doesn't care.

Half-formed ghosts twist before my eyes,
their features gradually becoming familiar.
Memories flood back,
of all the little things,
that made us best friends.

She always made me smile,
no matter what.
Through thick and thin,
she would always be there for me.

Now I may as well be invisible;
rejected and ignored.
Now she's gone, my life has fallen apart.
Leaving me in shreds.

We agreed never to part,
but you're not here anymore.
I hate to say this, but this is our end.

Rachel Haskell (13)

A TEENAGE THOUGHT!

Being a teen ain't so easy,
So many changes get on top of you,
Practising for GCSEs,
Emotions run wild,
Changes in your personal life,
You just want to scream, 'It's not fair!'

Entering a new year,
More studying and pressure all builds on your shoulders,
Emotions roll around your mind,
Areas of boredom, happiness, depression and aggression
All have a part in your mind.
So many changes it feels like a padlock without a key,
A wall is slowly built by all the characters in your life,
Adding a different chapter of pressure every day.

It feels like you want to take it slow,
Knock the wall down and realise they're only building blocks,
Made out of cheerful colours like red, green, orange and blue.
Understand how to control and cope,
Remember to take it day by day,
And start over with ABC and 123.

It all starts to become easy,
Making it ever so clear to see,
How much stress you put upon yourself,
Remember there's millions going through it right now!
It's as if you're not understood by the world,
But it's where you get to discover the real you,
Your interests and dislikes,
True friends are found,
Look ahead in your future and enjoy the times of a teenager.

You may feel lead on and confused by other peers,
But remember it's a phase of life where you find yourself.
I know it's hard, but it's only a stage,
The cycle of a busy little bee becoming a cheeky child,
Then into a teasing teenager all results in a young adult.
Remember to get through strong and look towards your busy life.

Courtney Gibbins (13)

LOVE IS NOT MY TRADE

To tell a story, that is my trade.
I work with words better used
To entice imagination where feelings fade.
Therefore, love should never be my trade.

I fail at its simple understandings
Yet see it all around me, abused.
It makes you do the stupid, the unthinkable,
Pushing the heart down onto heavy landings.

To speak my mind, that is my trade.
To spar with speech, targeting the tongue,
It gives me pleasure, something I'll happily parade.
Then again love would not be my trade.

It comes up with the greatest riddles,
The hardest of choices, recycled and reused.
Those experienced would know, alas not me –
I have the mind which dwindles.

To be ambitious, that is my trade.
Rising into recognition, excused.
My dreams are seldom made
Into love which plagues the trade.

Those who are professors
They take it lightly,
Achieving the small, the short.
They all see me as the lesser.

To judge before knowing, that is my trade.
Who am I to know something so infused?
When I detach myself from those who are not afraid
At love being their trade.

I'm a foal in a stable still afraid to see the sunshine,
I'm a monkey that laughs at his own reflection,
I'm a boy on receiving his first valentine,
I'm a man trying at his first affection,

Love is just my sleeping trade.

Harvey Lewis (18)

ONE, TWO, THREE

When I was ten, we played together,
Any game . . .
. . . Any weather

Our favourite game was hide-and-seek
Count to ten
And Dad don't peek
Quick! Under, inside and behind
Let's make it really tricky, make sure I'm hard to find

This is the best game, I'm having so much fun
Even if he finds me
I know I've already won

Oh no! I hear footsteps
I think he's coming near
Slowly take my breaths
He might know I'm here

Wait it's Mom . . . How did she find my place?
I've got to hide someplace else
Before he sees my face

Oh no! He sees me, now I have to seek
So I start counting
One, two, three

I hear a loud scream, then no one seemed to talk
My mom's calling me downstairs
But I'm too afraid to walk

Afraid to take that step, to down . . . there
When I walk in
The room is filled with tears

'Mom I have to play,'
But my mom didn't speak
The she choked the words
'I'm sorry dear, this is one hide you cannot seek.'

She told me it was okay to cry
Because it shone our feelings like a beam
It shows her that you were real

And not just her favourite dream.

She told me you're not coming back
And I would never find you whole
She told me you'd gone to a better place
And you'd lost your way back home.

But I know you're here somewhere,
Somewhere I can't see
So I'll keep on counting
One . . . two . . . three . . .

Prabjoat Layal (15)

THE GALE

Blindness in this thick fog
Only a myth, a story retold
At the heart of our fears
Disappointment causing tears

Words from the heart obscured
So much patience can endure
Shadows cast upon this tale
Doubts become a rushing gale

Weakness never an option
An impossibility by definition
Happiness is the ghost of yesterday
Losing the light and finding yourself astray

What may be the cause of this dismay
The crushing weight, the need for escape
Why does this heart cry with sorrow
With the invisible wounds of a widow.

Julia Greenwood (15)

HUNGER

This is hunger. An animal –
all fangs and eyes.
It cannot be distracted or deceived.
It is not satisfied with one meal.
It is not content
with a lunch or a dinner.
Always threatens blood.
Roars like a lion, squeezes like a boa,
thinks like a person.

The specimen before you
was captured in India
but it exists in a more or less savage state
in many other places.

Please stand back.

Jordhi Nullatamby (13)

WHERE AM I?

He stole every breath,
Trapped within a box,
Nothing in there with him,
Nothing but a key lock.
Despair and fear filled his heart.
This is something that he did not want to play the part.
Teardrops raced down his face,
Then he looked through the awkwardly shaped keyhole,
This was a strange, horrific place.
Not one tree, animal or plant caught his eye,
With only one question, running through his head,
Where am I?

Marley Martin (13)

EVER FEEL YOU'RE ALONE

Inside I'm crying
Outside I'm smiling
Thoughts racing through my head
Then come the tears I'm afraid to shed
Which I think should be put to bed

Nobody notices, until the anger fills my mind
With me being my only friend
I must be blind
It doesn't look like it but I want to die
Sadness, anger and unbearable pain

No one understands
All I need is a helping hand
As time moves slower
My self-esteem gets lower.

Ihsaan Rehman (14)

LIFE

Life is all about challenges, fun and pain.
We have friends who are here for life but some come and go.
There are times in our lives when we should look back on the past,
as a point of reference but think positive about the future.
There are people in this world that will hate you for your achievements,
but never let them stop you from achieving your goals.
Obstacles will be in your way, but if you trust in the Lord
with all your heart you will be just fine.
Life is too short to be dwelling on the past so,
Live like there's no tomorrow.
Love everyone you meet but learn from your mistakes.
Live life to the max because,
It will be worth it in the end.

Decodie Nicola Fisher (14)

NOT AGAIN?

Eyes open.
Yawning. Stretch.
Ah, lovely.
Sit up in bed.
Another day, another week, another chance, a way to be alive.
Ah, lovely.
Swing my feet over the edge of my bed.
Slip my feet into my slippers, soft and warm.
Lovely.
Peer at my reflection in the mirror.
Comment on how tired I look.
Not so lovely.
Apply some mascara. That's better.
Stumble downstairs.
Yawning again.
Eat some breakfast. Munch crunch. Nom nom.
Make my way to our main table.
Plonk myself down. Slurp some herbal tea.
Ah . . . lovely.
Start to sketch.
I love to draw. The way it calms me. The way it takes away all the stresses and the troubles, and replaces them with happiness.
Nothing can ever go wrong . . . !
Snap out of my bubble. Back to reality.
A younger sibling at the doorway, chatting on her phone.
And wearing my new clothes.
I'm seeing red.
It's worse than when I lost followers on Instagram.
I notice newly formed stains on the T-shirt.
I go berserk. Literally.
Snatch her mobile, throw it onto the carpet. Yell in frustration.
Little sis is crying now.
'Accident!' she says.
'Didn't know they were yours!' she says.
Mum comes in. Dad too.
'Don't yell like that.'
'You'll break her phone.'
I notice little sis smirking at me from the cover of the door.

Mum catches sight of her in the mirror.
Haha. She gets told off. Now it's my turn to grin.
I get spotted too. Sent to my room.
Sweeter words I have not heard spoken.
Umm . . . lovely?
So.
Every day is a gift (apparently)
Live it,
Love it,
And like it on Facebook!

Life is a slogan.
Right?

Angel Morrison-Parry (13)

PUPPET'S PLAY

It's another day.
Another day where this puppet must play his part.
Do as you're told; follow and obey.
Lie to yourself, lie to your heart.
Hide the sorrow with a simple smile.
Hide the pain of your heart's missing piece.
Those you hate, you must now admire.
And your love for others will simply cease.
Dance along in their little game.
Be the marionette you always were,
Whilst you suffer and writhe in pain,
But don't worry, to others, it's obscure.
It's another day.
Another day where this puppet must play his part.
Do as you're told; follow and obey.
Lie to yourself, lie to your heart.

Cameron Vincent (14)

OUR VERY OWN MONSTER

I wear my pride in abundance;
The heavy cloak lifting not weighing me down.
My only armour against her,
For she is ever ravishing and ever present.
She spouts sickly sweetness tempting me into her arms,
But then brushes me off and stamps me down when I dare stand defiant.
She is clever and cunning,
Wrapping me round her spiteful fingers.
Pushing me to the very edge,
Where everything stabs me in the chest.
My heart pulsating as my pride is ripped out with her words and ways.
What if I jump, if I leave this world by pushing myself over the edge,
My unforgiven mistakes and imperfections gnawing away at me?
She calls out.
She acts and dramatises as if I was her beloved;
She uses her spiteful, deceitful words declaring to the world I was 'cherished',
The very same world in which she tortured me,
In which she manipulated me and injected pressure into my boiling blood.
The pressure to be perfect.
But what would she say if I didn't jump, if I stay on this world.
If my soul squeezed my heart and said listen to it?
She would spit daggers into my conscience,
Burning venom-tipped daggers seeping her rules and regulations into my blood,
Moulding me like clay into something I am not nor will ever be.
Stretching me as if I were elastic, her evil gaze craving the jutting bones and sunken eyes.
She would continue blasting stereotypes in my face,
The deafening beat of injustice and my very own insecurity strangling my bruised soul.
My young, fledgling soul still learning the trade,
The trade of life.
We are the ones who have created this witch.
Gifted her with poisonous toxin for her cauldron of lies and fear.
Concocted the potion with our very words.
Past generations look at your hands!
Are they clean while you point at us accusingly?

We have created her for the future to be born into,
Where she will snap at her heels revoltingly with her malicious prejudice-soaked words.
Sinking into their souls treasuring the sickening sweet taste of pain.
There will be times when our children will think,
Why? Why are we convicted to the claws of this monster?
Because that's what they are: convicted, unable to escape, to break out of this mould.
What will you do to help our children;
I'll tell you what you'd do, what you done to us.
You would judge them.
For she has drilled it into our brains; and we have become it,
What she craved, exactly what she wanted; to become her.
For are we not all her? Therefore we are the monster.

All she does is label and judge us,
Every stigma attacked pierces through our existence.
We must change her if our children stand a chance.
We will try with all our might not to succumb, but to succeed.
We are souls who will not give up till every last breath has been extracted;
Every last tear shed.
Because too many vast waterfalls have crashed into the ground,
Raw. Painful. Those tears will cause the ground to shatter.
So let's make it worthwhile.
Let's cause her to shatter.
Let's break the moulds,
Destroy the blood soaked cages we have been decreased to.
We must be hurt today for our children to be free tomorrow,
Free of everything wrong with her.
Let's obliterate our world of this menace, replace it with something worthy,
Worthy to conduct humanity in all its glory.
We have been blaming for her too long.
For we are her, we are society.
So to morph this monster into an angel,
We must change ourselves first.
Let's define society.
Let it be a monster.
Our very own monster.

Sara Moufeed (13)

MY SECRET IS YOU

Everyone has a secret
I have one too
Most of my friends know,
But do you?
I can't explain what I'm feeling
I think this is true?
I'm not sure, I am falling for you
This is possible
Never knew that the feeling I had over you,
Would grow
I am falling for you
I'm falling once again
But, this time it's you,
I know this feeling
I had it before,
But, that was different
Because, she walked out through the door
I could be losing
But, I'll let the rain pour
Because, a day without you,
Is like hitting the floor
All over again
I'll fight this war
We are in the same class, with you behind me
Sitting there feels right
But, something's wrong
The rhyme is off
But, I'll sing this song
Because, it's beautiful and melody is lonely
Somehow it doesn't belong
It doesn't have to be perfect
So, why don't you sing along?
I'll be honest
I can believe that you were the one to make me come out of my shell
My friends know it and seen it
But, I'm like whatever
Being around you or just thinking of you
Makes me stupid

Can't you tell?
My friends know, but do you?
You think I'm funny from the little chats we have in our class
Do I have to spell it?
I'm telling you, I'm falling for you . . .
Do you feel the same as well?
I told you the truth,
So no I go
Unless you stop me
I'll leave you alone
Say you feel the same
Because, I don't want to be alone
I like you for you
And I know I don't need a wishbone
So I'll give you this
And hopefully, I won't kiss it goodbye
Know me, I'll probably dismiss the event
Because in all reality
I'm too intimidated, but I can't miss
Another chance to tell you the truth
I love you.

Danial Zabir (15)

WHY, WHY ME?

Why me? Why do I have nothing to give to this world?
People tell me I have talent, then why do I feel I have nothing?
People tell me I'm their 'backbone',
So why is it that whenever I do something wrong, I get told to 'get lost'?
I'm useless, I know it . . . no one understands me,
My feelings, my life, everything I do
Is being controlled by the two people I love most,
I say I don't love them, I know I don't help them, but I try my best, I do,

If they tell me what to do I will do it.
Only one thing I ask from them, you should ask them to,
All I need is love, that parental love . . .

What is that friendship? You know that one in school?
We were a variety of four, one was sweet, the other spicy,
Another was sleek, and then there's me sitting secluded,
But like they say always think positive, so I do and I think 'opposites attract',
It worked, until you find one of your 'friends' have lied to your face,
But I try, I do, to try and work it out, ditto, so ask that question why, why me?

Ahaa! Jealousy . . . the work of the devil most would say.

Can we always blame Mr Fire?
That character most believe in,
Would we take all our troubles out on him if I told you a short story?
Well here goes and listen carefully, this is why Mr Fire won a BAFTA,
See if we can blame him after . . .
Along came Mr Fire, his cunning suit and basket of fruit . . .
Mr Fire looks human, his basket looks healthy.
What is that I see? A block of bubbly cheese?
He took out his cheese and placed it on the floor,
Along came the mouse, so hungry and weak,
But before it could eat, along came two screeching cats.
One cat eliminated the other in reward for the mouse,
Before the cat could consume the mouse,
A man witnessed this incident and therefore banished that cat
From this earth. His fellow neighbour witnessed the banishing
Of his own cat and dispatched the notorious neighbour
From the world . . .
To this day two families are at war,

Because Mr Fire placed a piece of cheese on the crooked floor . . .

Can I blame others around me? Or do I have to change?
Every day I know, I *will* try, I *will*,
But still ask that question why, why *me*?

Husna Boksh (14)

THE LOST FLOWER

Walking barefooted on a thorny field for the search
Of the lost flower, on a winter afternoon.
She doesn't stop but walks, her love is too thick to understand.
Blisters popping, skin crackling, blood oozing but she still walks, walks for the lost flower.
There's hope, always hope, the red passionate rose has its
Sharp-like thorns to protect its beauty flower,
Lucky it must be to have her walking, looking, searching.
Late leaves falling, cramped on, stepped on, despite it had its own flower
Dead and gone.
But she's still walking, for the flower she lost. She is looking for me.
Frosty and cold, do I stand alone, waiting,
Because she's the only one who waters me,
A mother's voice is one of maternal tenderness,
It feeds me to be alive.
The journey long, far too long, whimpering, falling,
But she still is walking on a thorny field barefooted,
Only because Mother love is not based on distance.

Sadiah Khanum (16)

IT'S JUST A REFLECTION

The feeling of irrelevancy and disappointment is not the greatest
but a side effect of being a nobody to a somebody that is more worthy than you will ever be.
Even though I have a thin glass wall wrapped around me,
others are still able to break in and chain me between the earth and the heavens in such a joyful manner.

I fear the world full of tears and laughter within,
I fear the love as it descends upon us all,
I fear the value of life without the scent of the loved ones,
but I will never fear the misinterpretation and misjudgment I have adapted myself to survive by.

They ask me why the hesitation and weakness,
but I reply with a face full of strength.
A strength that became mine after I fell every twilight,
but a strength that explodes into delicate tulip petals in a field sugar-coated with acceptance.

I wake up stronger and prepared
as the pain and loneliness enters every inch of my skin
I can't help but enjoy the pleasure of the numbness I have allowed my body to re-enter.
But what's the point if I keep looking away.

Every time I see it,
it's just a small reminder of what I really am,
who I really am,
and the reason behind my unjustifiable silence.

As my heart starts to pump out every word that has stung me,
my brain interprets them into such a cold song.
I begin to slowly embrace a dance to the new beat
but I then realise I'm falling too deep.

The thick black liquid trickles from my head to toe in such a jiggered line,
proving that I will never have my ups but I will always have my downs.
So I look up as tears well in my eyes
and wish to land on a cold hard ground so I can rest my stoned head and pray.

Every moment I wish I can just fly far away.

Allow myself to be swept by the nature of the colourless wind.
Me and just my black wings.
Whilst they carry my body as I shield them from all the hatred that they are still yet to receive.

Amani Ahmed (15)

MY DAD

I once had a daddy,
A daddy strong and tall,
He was my knight in shining armour,
The one who'd never let me fall.

But then my dad got poorly,
Then slowly worse and worse,
Soon enough he couldn't move,
His system falling into reverse.

But then he did seem better,
We could still laugh and talk,
He was still my daddy,
Even though he could not walk.

Then suddenly he was ill again,
This time worse than before,
It was clear he wasn't getting better,
And this chilled me to the core.

I really miss you Daddy,
I miss the fun times that we had,
Because even though you're not with me,
You'll always be my dad.

Eliza Worden (14)

THIS IS MY LIFE, MY TEENAGE LIFE

I'm confused about life
my friends don't seem to understand me
friends nitpicking at me
family supporting me through the tough times
but what they don't see
is the pain in my eyes
and the fake smile on my face
covering up the painful sensation.
This is my life, my teenage life.

I take it all out on Mum and sister
but I don't mean to
I am sorry for all the pain I have put you through
but don't blame me
it's my 'so-called friends' that irritate me
but somehow, I take it out on you.
This is my life, my teenage life

Then the next day comes
and it is the total opposite of yesterday
everyone there, talking including me
they ask 'what's wrong?' when I am happy
but when I am sad, they don't give a damn.
This is my life, my teenage life.

Shannon Sellars (14)

THESE DAYS

We don't know what we're feeling,
Are we lost or okay?
We feel like we're the only ones in this world,
Are we alone or altogether?
We get jealous of little things,
Are we crazy or normal?
We get bored of doing nothing,
Are we lame or cool?
We're and we're down,
Are we on a roller coaster or still?
We think lyrics are the only ones there for us,
Is it comforting or upsetting?
We don't know what we are going to do with our lives,
Are we speechless or smart?
We're worried and happy at the same time.
Are we happy or sad?
We feel pressured by society
Are we stressed or depressed?
We think the way we look is important,
Is it really or is it not?
We are the teens of today and we're just growing up.

Sima Jaf (15)

A TEEN JUST LIKE ME . . .

I feel happiness,
I feel rage,
Sometimes I just need to be let alone in a cage.
When I'm happy,
All I see is the sun,
And all I do is,
Hum,
Hum,
Hum!

There is so many emotions one teenager can feel,
Sometimes I just feel like a jumble sale,
Anger,
Rage,
Happiness,
And joy
They all build up inside of me,
There's a lot a simple smile can hide,
But true feelings are only revealed,
When the mask is lifted . . .

You can't just tell by looking at me,
You can't just ask me what's wrong.
All these things are sealed up inside of me,
I'm a caterpillar becoming a butterfly . . .
Everybody wants happiness,
Nobody wants pain,
But you can have a rainbow,
Without a little rain . . .

Anjali Gupta (13)

SINGULARITY

Glass houses and towers kissed by the rays
Of the sun as it rises at dawn,
Lighting crystal streets, setting all ablaze
In memory of the city that burned.

Glass windows, glass streetlights glow in the day,
As a city should glow at night,
And every floor is tinged with grey,
As darkness bleeds up from below.

I am the dark shape which fell through the sky,
I am the tears, the panic and the screams.
I am the impact, the heat, I vaporised
Their corpses, their homes and their dreams.

Children to ashes and ashes to glass
In the rage of my tyranny,
As wide eyes, dry mouths and quivering hearts
Were shredded and scattered with glee.

Alone. With their faces stained on my eyes
And their shrieking alive in my head.
Alone. As their city dies and dies
In my mind, as I live in their stead.

So I built upon the ashen ground
And hid the blackened past,
Yet the dark is there, and can be found
Through my city made of glass.

These many floors of melted stone,
Their cracks and chips and holes,
Cannot obscure the wretched home
Of countless weeping souls.

Memory hurts, but I can't feel
The pain I yearn to share
With the dead, whose wounds I cannot heal,
Whose bones I can't repair.

Kieran Kejiou (17)

ANGELS

Angels, dancing and singing in the sky,
Good morning, and good night,
I'm guessing you'll be gladly returning,
Coming to me when I need it – when I am mourning, dwelling, yearning,
Dreams of the impossible in my mysterious mind,
Nothing at all, left to hide,
Angels, see crystal clear, right through me,
I know, them, look – see.

So angels, angels,
Rise up onto the glorious heavens,
I can't believe it with my own eyes,
We are floating on thin air,
And I wouldn't dream to dare,
Angels, all I dream,
Angels is all I just happen and seem to see,
Angels in the sky,
So high,
Angels fly, fly.

In that heavenly, beautiful sky,
What can you, and do you see,
Down here on Earth,
Every single traumatic death, every single memorable birth,
This all goes round in a circle,
The true sincerity,
Of their fragile hearts,
Don't they ever break apart,
Protecting their own wellbeing,
I'll be definitely seeing,
You, my angels.

So angels, my angels,
Rise up onto the glorious heavens,
I can't believe it with my own eyes,
We are floating on thin air,
And I wouldn't dream to dare,
Angels, all I dream,
Angels is all I just happen and seem to see,
Angels in the sky,

So high,
Angels, fly, fly.

I'll be looking and searching, right out there on the rooftops,
For you, my dear angels,
I'll be sitting down out there in the cold night, twinkling starlight,
For you, my dear angels,
I'll be smiling out there, in the eye of the dull moonlight,
For you, my dear angels,
I'll be thinking out there, in the mist, in the fog, in the rain,
For you, my dear angels,
I'll be kind out there, be true to myself, be true to you,
For you, my dear angels,
I'll be singing out there, with my heart, and my soul, and my all,
For you, my dear angels
I'll be everything out there, you want me, to be,
For you, my dear angels!

So angels, angels,
Rise up onto the glorious heavens,
I can't believe it with my own eyes,
We are floating on thin air,
And I wouldn't dream to dare,
Angels, all I dream,
Angels is all I just happen and seem to see,
Angels in the day and night sky,
So high,
Angels fly, fly.
Fly, sky high,
Fly, fly,
Fly, fly,
Fly, fly . . .
Angels fly . . .

Arveen Kaur Graya (14)

ANNA

Anna is only young,
She does not understand the world that keeps her prisoner.
Anna does not understand why her land has turned to sand.
Why men fight, and die.
Or why her family is gone . . . Gone where?
Anna would like to know.
Anna is only young and does not understand . . .
But Anna is special.
Anna is braver than any lion.
Stronger than any ox.
Sharper than any eagle.
And has a heart that still beats alone in her chest,
Blood still in her veins and tears still bled from her eyes.
She is stronger than you,
Braver than me and sharper than us all.
Anna is young and she understands.
She understands that bullets destroy lives and wars burn nations.

But knowing doesn't always keep people alive.
Anna is gone now,
She is strong but not strong enough to face metal and rock.
Her grave was the road and her roses, bullets.
But Anna understood.

Tim Thornton (17)

THE UNDERGROUND

There I was,
In the darkness
Screeching sounds and empty echoes.

Deafening screams,
Black surrounding me
Only until my eyes decoded the way did I see.

The hollow everlasting pipe,
Ancient black arches
Wires attached to each side.

I minded my step for the ground seemed unstable,
I tripped over a pebble,
Falling against the side again.

Then it came,
The high screech was louder
I leaned back; aghast.

The tunnel was lit up,
The screams were produced by a train
The white and red draped against its skin.

I don't know how I got there,
The pounding in my head didn't help
The black memories were blurred.

Alexia Jeayes

CHANGE

It's horrible and strange,
but I guess I have to change.
There's a new me bursting out,
even though I'm still in doubt.

Everything's really weird,
all the boys will get a beard.
I know that we have to grow,
now my feelings are on overflow.

I feel really odd,
like I should join the football squad.
We've all changed,
my body's been rearranged.

I feel so irregular,
I've never been popular.
We're not all the same,
but life is one big game.

Morgan Hill (13)

HARMFUL

He knew a girl who liked to draw,
She drew pictures that nobody saw.
She was more artistic alone at night,
In her bedroom out of sight.
She didn't tell a soul and the gallery grew.

They had a date, down by the river, under the stars,
She rolled up her sleeve and showed him her scars.
She was so embarrassed, she looked at her shoe,
He rolled up his sleeve and said, 'I draw too.'

Sophie Pollintine (13)

UNTITLED

I have decided
that books are not real.
Life is not like that;
The girl doesn't get the boy, the world
is not saved, or destroyed either.
Everyone is not beautiful and good.
You don't save my life, and
I don't save yours.
You don't kiss me in the rain
because you don't exist.
I am not funny, fierce, courageous,
dazzling, wise, beautiful,
just confused.

Freya Thorpe

AN IDEAL WORLD

There is a world in my eye,
Yes, of course with green and blue skies,
But where the friends don't tell lies,
Where the lovers stay real,
And the smiles give the warmth to heal

The parents keep the arguments to a few,
The DVDs given to me are also new,
Games are all mine,
Even the food is fine,
Burgers with chips or fries, all at their demise

There is a world in my eye,
But even if it did come true,
We'd all call it a lie.

Daniel Link (17)

THE UNDERSTANDING

We say 'no one understands' because no one does understand
It's difficult to stand and say and say with vindication that we understand the plight of the other
We all live in our little bubbles of denial
We reside in restricting cocoons
In which the truth is shunned
Why?
We're too afraid to accept it
Too afraid of the bitterness of everything around us
Consumed by our own dilemmas and predicaments
We claim to understand each other
But we all lie
We do not live, for our lies are the sword that strikes us all
And the coldness of our hearts freezes our emotions
Leaving us lost and delusional
Our vision is so blurred we miss the fine line between love and hate
We can no longer distinguish between right and wrong
Life is a figment of our imagination, a disease that does nothing but bring disappointment wrapped in silk bows and roses
But we don't see it
No one understands
No one understands
No one ever did
No one ever will
Not even me.

Tatenda Gandi

UNTITLED

I wanted to sing, that's all I had learnt,
I wanted to know, your hands were stinging with hurt,
From clapping so loud and cheering so wild,
Like a bull in a ring or a tiger in the wild.

All I had known, was I had gone astray,
From those that I used to know,
In a long lost day, those that knew,
Every word on a page, every sum was so simple,
Yet I felt trapped in a cage.

Yes they'd understand everything they had learnt,
Yet all I could see, was my future red and burnt,
For you I was sunshine, yet I was not bright,
Yet you were always shining, both day and night.

They knew how I was, but I was so lost in a crowd,
I just wanted to pass and for you to be proud,
I will need time, even when you have power,
Whilst you'll spend a minute, I'll spend an hour.

I wanted to sing, that's all I had learnt,
In my mind, in my heart,
Something you can never be taught.

Brontë Leia Hardy (15)

A CITY OF DREAMS . . .

Like a fairy tale . . .

The rivers were crystal clear like rare gems; shining beautifully in the night.
If you touch the water in the rivers, you will feel that it is as cool and calm as a midsummer's breeze.
And when it is night, there is no need of lights or electricity
. . . The stars are your light, which light up the cities.
With one glance at these luminous, celestial lights,
You will fall into an exotic daze; far off the realms of imagination.

The streets of these heavenly paradises were more divine than gold, silver and diamond combined!
Do you know why this is?
It is because, when you walk on the pavements
It's like a vision of ecstasy.
But it doesn't end there!
The buildings and skyscrapers are like
Stalagmites; they tower high above over everything.

Whereas, the sun is the guardian of these sublime cities;
He watches over everyone like a shepherd guarding its sheep . . .

Paa Kofi Kyereh

INCREDIMAZABLE

A ball of rage filled my heart,
As I knew me and Chloe would soon depart.
My once close friend, as white as snow,
Would come back a tiger, ready to blow.
A soft kitten with a peculiar taste,
Would be no more, nature would take its place.
A transformation of a cat to a tiger,
Was no big deal to me, it was a minor.
I was selfish, impatient and insecure,
For I knew my Chloe would be no more.
From the way she purred, to the way she drank her milk,
And would hide, in case her fur was used as a mink.
But she would grow a tiger, big and strong,
With much fur and legs three metres long.
She'd run from the poachers, duck and dive,
My Chloe would be alive.
The transformation of a cat to a tiger, living life to the full,
Only one way to describe it;
Incredimazable.

Tomi Olurebi

IT'S SIMPLY AN ADVENTURE CRYING OUT FOR YOU

I like to think of life as a huge roller coaster.
Life is simply beyond the human imagination.
You will never predict what is to become of you,
Until the door opens to release you into the world of wilderness.
Never under estimate the human body or mind.
Never let anyone tell you that you are bad
Or need to be more like someone else,
At the end of the day you are who you are that's the most important thing in life.

Teenage years . . . I guess . . . can be stressful,
Emotionally draining and frustrating.
But it's an adventure crying out for you.
Always think positive, no matter what happens.
Teenage life is filled with happiness, contentment and joy.
Before, I end this poem here . . . remember:
'Never regret anything that has happened in your life.
It cannot be changed, undone or forgotten
So take it as a lesson and move on.'

Esme Barrett-Lamb (14)

GUARDIAN ANGEL . . .

My guardian angel, that's what he is
With his wings made of pure black, promising strength
And his promises, his words, his love
His love fooled me, he blinded my judgment
I was another one of his mortal toys
Someone help me, my guardian angel ripped out my heart
My guardian angel, that's what he was

Sleepless nights, thinking of him
Yearning for the intensity of his eyes
The warmth reminding me of pity, love and care
They flooded my senses with desire
And then he would smile and my world would be whole once again
He was one of a kind
My guardian angel, that's what he was

My guardian angel, someone tell me, where is he now?
He snatched my heart, my soul and my entire reason to exist and left
Left me to be swallowed in an endless torrent of agony
Pure, raw, sheer pain
My heart's breaking, not bearing the thought that he is no longer mine

My guardian angel, that's what he is and will always be.

Thaiba Ayub (15)

ROSE GARDEN

Red, pink, white
You could fly a kite
Alice painted them
And got the paint on her skirt hem

Rose garden
Where Alice says, 'Pardon?'
A rose represents love
But you need to wear a glove

The colour red, looks like they've bled
After time they end up dead
The colour pink, will make you blink
Watch out for the ink

Alice took a drink
Which made her shrink
The Mad Hatter
Was full of chatter

His tea
Made you fill with glee.

Rebecca Barnwell (15)

WAITING ON THE EDGE OF THE WORLD

Once again I fear of awakening, in a world of tortured sweetness.
What I have seen and what I have heard, heart break does not greet you lightly
Each day is long as I long for each day, and each hour becomes a minute, of every day.

The life I long, passes through my fingertips,
And yet I see still not, in my longing eye, the one I wish to see.
For too long I have waited, too long I have watched,
And now the sun shall be rising, and greet me with a burning kiss.

My heart feels like a cup of un-drunk love that waits for the first gulp.
For these stars do wish to be seen, as I do also,
And as I pass through a tear of salty hate, I find what had been hidden.

Beauty till now it has been hidden from one boy's heart,
And as I stand next to him he says to me;
'What till now have my eyes been hiding, for now I that can see, my heart can give its love'
Then as the world, moon and stars reveal themselves, I fall in love and into his arms,
At last!

Lael Carlton

A POEM FOR PIRATES

Y'all be trapped in the locker
Of the devilish Davy Jones
The beast will gobble ye up
And spit out all ye bones!

Y'all be sailing the open seas
Scrubbing the deck,
Y'all be on ye knees
Buccaneers set the sails free
You're nothing but a pirate!
And a pirate is all you can be!

To be a pirate
You don't need treasure or greed
A bottle of rum is all ye need
Yo ho ho
To Tortuga we go!

Men of the mast are a loyal crew
If you're not loyal they'll be after you
Ye better be warned if you're a captain at sea
Treat the men right, or there'll be a mutiny!

Connor Sheffield (18)

EMOTIONS

Anger – raging, stomping, heavy breathing, pupils dilating
Calmness – soothing, slowing, light breathing, anger fading
Tiredness – yawning, sitting, quiet breathing, images fading
Happiness – jumping, smiling, loud breathing, body awakening.

Ryan Malzard (14)

LOOK WHAT YOU'VE DONE

You know it hurts,
One word becomes ten,
Fat, ugly, worthless,
These are the words they can say,
You see them crying again and again,
'Ha ha, you're gay,' you say.

The pain you've caused will get too much,
This girl; my close friend can no longer cope,
'It hurts, it hurts,' she cries with such a gentle blush,
'You're a loser,' you yell but you don't realise she has lost all hope.

The sharp knife sinks as she bursts her skin,
The bright red blood flows right out,
'Get a grip your trash bin bowling pin,'
She lies there on the floor, she doesn't know what to say anymore.

As she lies bleeding on the floor,
She couldn't be helped anymore,
Look what you've done you bully,
She'll never ever move a muscle,
What can I do now?

The police sirens blaring,
I just seem to break down,
Her mum was crying and swearing,
I sat in my old dressing gown,
Before I knew it a policeman was by my side,
I can't believe she's gone. It's all because of you,
I can't believe she actually died . . .

Lindsey Reid (14)

FRIENDS IN LIFE

What is life?
Life is but a box
Deep, dark, depressing
In which friends lock.

These so-called friends
Lie and cheat to survive
They have damaged me so much
That I cannot be perceived.

They stole my trust
They are like thugs
Things in the darkest of nights
They always wear the smile of smug.

However I love them
I need to forget
But they will do it again
My trust they will neglect.

Ryan Fallon (14)

FLESH AND BONE

How can one be so confident and strong, in their own flesh and bone
Then begin to slowly disintegrate under the pressure
Lose themselves and become just as a leaf in the wind
Lost with no way of finding where you came from
Lost, with no possible way of having things the way they used to be

My heart hurts and I can't be on my own,
Why me?
I feel the crumbling sensation coming over me again,
Falling apart, bit by bit, falling back into the ditch that I just got out of.
Black.
Darkness.

Eunice Otoo (16)

TEENAGE BLUES

I'm not going to write about love, but not because I've never been heartbroken,
I'm not going to write about hate, as I haven't learnt to forgive and forget,
I'm not going to write about trust, although I have once trusted the wrong people.

I'm not going to write about those, who once laughed but now cry,
I'm not going to write about the young adults, who once smiled but now frown and
I'm not going to write about the ones, who were once determined but gave up and let their dreams die.
So now you ask, what will I write about?

I will write about the mistakes we teenagers stupidly make.
A mistake is a purpose which challenges and changes your emotions;
It affects your imagination but at the same time strengthens your focus.

Chisanga Mwila (13)

STICKS AND STONES

We all have grown up hearing it,
We've all been told it's true.
'Sticks and stones may break your bones but words will never hurt you'.
It was all a lie, what we heard was wrong,
We weren't told of the hatred that could torrent off a tongue.
That a simple sentence made of words could make us feel so scared,
Could make me feel alone, feel like nobody else cared.
So we lock ourselves away from life, hide underneath the bed,
Spend countless nights just thinking, thoughts spinning round your head.
You believe what they're saying, it starts to all make sense.
Your life is not reality, your smile is a pretence.
They target all your weaknesses, it's hurting in your heart,
You know that . . .
Sticks and stones may break your bones, but words will tear you apart.

Helena Schoner (15)

THE PHANTOM ANGEL

The glimpse of a girl
Surely a trick of the light
The blink of an eye
She had faded into the night
And then they would ponder
Who it could be?
That haunted their minds
Yet their eyes couldn't see?
Could it be the one?
Promised to save them all
Biding her time
As she watched their tears fall?
But time wasn't stopping
The pain was still there
Eating away at them
Driving them to the heights of eternal despair
The sun shined brightly
The day brand new
The torture endless
The victims now few
To wash away their fears . . .
Oh how she longed to save them from their evil fate!
To unlock her heart
Let her love devour its hate
The might of this beast
As it crushed their hearts with its power
And let them fall into the blood-red soils
Like the seeds of a flower
Their time now up
Their ends very near
The kiss of death
The ultimate fear
And still she watched them
Their souls now devoured
Their guardian angel
Nothing more than a coward.

Haleema Hussain (16)

MORNING RASPBERRIES

This morning could snap me in half;
so hardened and crisp, it pinches me
Blades of grass break from their frosty cocoons,
wingless wicks from white candles

Pools of yellow give weak warmth –
I bask between them, sometimes crossing
into the unbearable shade,
but linger little.

The ground is not yet molten
but the sky's furnace flames.
An armada rages on the horizon,
and all lights from port.
The shepherds will heed their warning
This morning.

The sky warns the raspberries below
she knows her morning garb will fade
so will their crimson uniforms.
Unless I pick soon

the berries' colour will imitate the afternoon
then dye to the night's inky cloak.
I must pick today.
Beauty before age,
or all goodness fades.

Camilla Bell-Davies (18)

MY HAIR

My hair was long before I was ten
By the time I got to twelve it was all gone again
I dyed it brown and I dyed it blonde
And now it's gone all wrong
So I get it cut to make it right and it just goes green
Like I have come off a flight.

Harriet Palmer (14)

THE GREAT AND POWERFUL SEA

My old song sings again
A song of millenniums
It never stops you see
That constant crash
That constant swish
Forever playing on repeat
People used to fear me
I was more powerful than Poseidon
My incredible pull
I filled the night terrors on those sad small ships
Not now
I used to force them in
Make them suffer
Make them mine
But I'm no longer cruel
They come willingly now
They don't scream or fight or pray
They enjoy my constricted hold
Finding peace within my ever going body
Like children
They dive into my depths
Sometimes I play
Throwing them in and out of my coldness
But sometimes I just watch
They soon turn limp
Cold as me now
Hidden in my depths
That 95% of unknown liquid
That's me
Sometimes I let them go
Push them back
But not always

I preserve them
Tie them within the very soul of myself
Now they are part of me
It's sad, I know
But they are just a sad twisted soul
Forever in my need
The great and powerful sea.

Molly Lythaby (14)

EVERY NIGHT I TRY TO SLEEP

Every night I try to sleep
But I hear the bees buzzing
So I try to count sheep
But I hear the alarm ringing
I turn on my other side
But then the whistle blows
I ask whose playing these sounds
I demand their name at once
It's 3am in the morning
And all I want is sleep
There's a pillow on my ear
But the sound won't quieten
But I do eventually fall asleep
But the sounds keep playing on
And wakes me up too early
Between two to three hours later
It happens every day so I get ready
Ready for tonight's cycle again.

Joshua Teya (17)

LIFE OF A TEENAGER

Hustling and bustling,
Hanging and gaming,
Pinging and linking,
Going to park to have a laugh,

That's the life of a teenager.

The stereotypes are becoming a reality,
Algebra and equations
Who does that?
Homophones and synonyms
Who knows that?
Eating with the parents,
Huh, *leave* that!

That's the life of a teenager.

Flicking a new page,
I'm finally out of that cage,
Now wondering how to get a wage,
All I needed to worry about is life ahead,
And make sure my dreams don't drop dead.

That's the life of a teenager.

High above I can see the sky,
Bright as day I can't tell a lie,
As the hectic day comes to an end,
I finally can rest my head,
In my sweet bed.

That's the life of a teenager.

Jahmal Taylor (13)

GROUNDHOG CHILDHOOD AND LIFE'S LONG QUEST

Some people say being a child is easy,
And they wish to go back
This gene in life I'm afraid I must lack . . .

It's only when I'm alone, can my true feelings come to light
Even through the world's bitterness and spite,
I know I'm gonna be alright
Yet the stars above me shine so bright
Even through the foggy autumn night.

I only see through the eyes of a child,
I have not experienced being wild or mature,
My mind's a sponge that absorbs more and more . . .

I have lots to learn this I know,
Plenty of time to bloom and grow,
So down the path of life I go . . .

Through bitterness, joy and life's bad deeds,
Deep down friendship and love is all a person needs.

When I grow from a boy to a man
I would have accomplished all that I can.

Emotions and feelings are a lot to bear,
But at fifteen I just don't care . . .

I'm living my childhood like I do best,
Full of fun and childhood zest
After all I'm only fifteen and innocence is all I've seen
So I will try my best till my time comes to rest.

Daniel Sadd (15)

BEAUTY AND THE BEAST

Beauty.
Her real story wasn't told,
They never mentioned how
The beast tore up her soul.

Her honey voice,
Would sing in the day,
But when darkness fell,
The beast would come and devour her like prey.

She'd wake up alone,
Not remembering a thing,
The only sign of evidence,
Were the scratches on her skin.

She would stagger away
Still in a daze,
She felt like her life was
Turning into a complicated maze.

She felt trapped.

But one day,
In the soft glow of the evening sun,
Her prince came riding,
Was he the one

To save her from this nightmare?

No. It was too late.

What was happening?
She didn't know.
The beast attacked,
Its eyes, they glowed.

The tearing of flesh.
The cracking of bone.
Beauty was lost in darkness,
Cold, frightened and alone.

Beauty screamed.
Wildlife fled.
The prince's mangled body,
Was lifeless. Dead.

Beauty cried,
Sobs racked her body.
She stared at her delicate hands,
They were shaking and bloody.

Beauty can be ugly,
Just as west can be mistaken for east,
There was simply no denying that,
Beauty was the beast.

Danielle Sojinrin (14)

WORLD OF ME

Hello world of poets, we've got so much alike,
But when we look closer, do we know what's wrong or right?

The world is a mystery, that's what people say,
I agree with this wholeheartedly, like you may.

My life is sometimes difficult, but it's sometimes really fun,
I have two darling sisters but we fight like everyone.

But what I have is special, I'm a triplet, one of three,
However, people think of 'the triplets', they never think of just me.

So can you see my reasoning, my life is good and bad,
I have many happy memories but I have a few that are sad.

I hope this poem helps, to understand the life of me,
But if you have a problem understanding it, the connection of triplets is the key.

Charlotte Elliott (13)

I DO . . .

When the sky turns blue
When all wishes come true
And you say 'I do'
I'll give you my hand
I'll give you my heart
I'll give you everything I've got

If the love is true
If the sky turns blue
I'll give you my life
I'll hand it to you
I'll share all my burdens
My troubles, my pains
I'll show you the way
I'll guide you to it

But only if you promise
To love me, to hold me
To never let go, to never forget

I'll love you forever
And that is a promise
The love we possess
Will guide us through it

But only when death comes
I'll tell you the truth
I'll tell you that death will not separate us
I'll tell you that I'll love you for eternity.

Alise Ziemele (14)

ME

Inside I feel I know it all
Outside I feel I am going to fall
Inside I could be crying
But outside I am trying

What do I do
Maybe it is true?
My heart skips a beat
As I walk up the street

Nobody understands me
I just want to be free
Everything is so confusing

Why do people give me 'that' look
As if I have come straight out of a book
Am I really that different
Or is it that I am special?

I don't know what to do
I just need to let it go
All I need is to know

I ask all around
What could it be
Maybe it is me?

Aayushi Dhawan (13)

MY EXPERIENCE WITH THE SUPERNATURAL

There are no such things as ghosts
I tell you.
At least that's what I thought
Until that weird and spooky day.
Listen close . . . I'll let you know a story
That is true.

I left school, compared to everybody else,
A little late.
I had a lot of work to finish,
To keep myself on track.
So my friends had gone home,
I had told them not to wait.

Unlike a usual school day,
The roads felt empty.
But somebody was definitely behind me,
I had hoped, not following, just going the same way.
I exclaimed to myself, 'Stop being a scaredy-cat
You numpty!'

I cornered to the right, then
Slowed down my pace.
Turning around, my heart
Was relieved,
After I saw a woman who walked
Right past me as though she was in a race.

'I could be *so* paranoid,' I laughed
As I opened the front door.
Just about to shut it when, there she was . . .
My ghost was one of my best friends
Who gave me such a fright,
I nearly dropped to the floor.

She told me how she did it,
Stalking me I mean.
We laughed about it and I told her
She was a professional.
Until that day, I believed
Ghosts weren't real.
I have never experienced them so I would still say,
'There are no such things as ghosts.'

Chidera Madukwe (15)

UNTITLED

Glaciers melted in her eyes, left unreturned and broken,
Swam into the iciest blank of the sea,
Which carried the dense lines where waves had parted.
A glance would follow a gaze,
Until the zephyr became a screeching cry echoing from the sky.
She washed in reds and bathed in soft pinks,
When dusk came, she was afloat a cloud,
And possessed a pocket watch,
I leant an ear to the drift of a tick,
It soothed her fragmented heart,
Whilst I folded sweet nectar into my mouth.
A balm of musk circled the thick cold air,
It lingered on me, whilst I followed her into an oasis.
Blissful tranquillity occupied it.
The adornment, I took pleasure in.
I am immersed in lucidity and she is also an enigma.

Henna Malik (13)

TWIST OF LOVE

You are my star, shining bright,
You guide me through the misty night,
You treasure my heart as a precious jewel,
Your love, a never-ending whirlpool.

Our vowels remain forever strong,
As I dismiss all your wrong,
You shot me this time, pistols of gold,
Leaving me wishing our relationship was bold.

But now you're not there to fix my heart,
After you shattered it apart,
So when I really need a friend, you
Said you'll be there in the end.

Now all I see are needles of light,
Through the cracks of my broken heart, held tight,
To tend me through this painful time,
All alone in a gold mine.

But time has gone of your destruction,
Now I read 'love for dummies' instructions,
You're the one, who locked me out,
But I'm not to plead and pout.

There will be a time, when I find Mr Right,
In shining silver armour, to guide me through the night,
He will be the lost piece of the jigsaw,
No matter his wealth, rich or poor.

If he protects my heart,
We will never be apart,
He will be ruby red,
My heart is not to be bled.

No money could buy it,
Nobody could steal it,
The world against it.

Kavita Kalyan (13)

HEROINE

I know a girl
Unlike any other
With a hard story
One does make me shudder
As its various winding histories
Stumble and collapse into each other
Reappearing within her life
Making themselves known.

I see her through public eye
A mask she holds to frame her frights
Of everlasting nightmares, she tries to escape
Which taunt her, making her cower.

The burden she holds on her shoulders
The experience of cruelty she's bound
Causes her to plaster a fake smile on her withered face
Acting passive in public space.

Never seeming attentive
But never fading out
Trying to keep unnatural balance
In her crumbling world of hell.
Her growing wish to make the past scarce
Her hushed screams to be heard
For her life's misery to be turned

Her old shouts were carried away by rough winds.
But her new screams get louder and louder.
Her stone heart burns with desire.
The solitary mind works alone
But for it to achieve its ambition
It must strive for greatness
She possesses the strength to make a difference
To be an inspiration
A heroine in the making.

Ranna Gadogbe

ITS . . .

Its thin wide lips,
Its crooked nose,
Its elf-like ears,
Its hairy mole sitting on its cheek,
Its brittle long jet black hair,
Its bony delicate, still face,
Its grey skin,
Its lifeless tear rolling down its face going 250 miles an hour,
Its cockeyed, small, red eyes dying inside with loneliness,
Its smiling face hiding in front of a puny, worthless creature,
Its pale purple nails, dead as hope,
Its cringe-worthy, backstabbing, scared smile,
Every Tom, Dick and Harry loathes 'it',
For 'it' has neither an ounce of good nor an ounce of truth,
'It' . . . is staring at me
'It' . . . is staring at me
'It' . . . is staring at me
Why is 'it' staring at me?
Why is it staring at me in the mirror?
For 'it' is me. *Ssshhhh!*

Nastexo Ahmed Nur (14)

TEENAGE YEARS

Teenage years;
They're full of fears,
Flooded with tears
And seem to go on for decades
Your parents don't get you,
Your crush resents you
And you go through friends like you do emotions!

But when you look back through your life on a rainy day,
You'll smile and think –
'Hey, my teenage years weren't all that grey!'

Christy Duvenhage (15)

EVERYTHING'S GONNA BE ALRIGHT

When you think you've had enough, because things get tough,
The fights,
Bad nights,
People being tight,
And you just wishing there was no tomorrow,
Just believe in yourself and borrow some happiness and smile,
Everything's gonna be alright, they may be tight,
But they're just not right,
Everything they say, every day, in the end, they will pay,
Karma will come, and they will be done,
No more bad feelings,
No more peelings on yourself,
Even though you wanna say goodbye forever
And never see the bullies and tears again!
Just put the bottle down and just tell everyone how you feel,
Yes they may judge but everything's gonna be alright, just remember.

Megan Blest (13)

A CHEAT

Lips fleered back, baring those white set of teeth.
A magnanimous personality also.
A chambray was always placed on the end of the bed,
A fine linen slipping against the left leg.
Quite a few toils were around, a collection maybe.
Most was a gingham fabric.
The night condenses into her, allays the bonds of her serotonin blight.
Once they speak, they just seem to meander on,
Always listening attentively, with the perfect response.
But when fallen for, she twists, turns and unable to stand again,
Secretly a liar and a cheat.
We women are fools.

Kelsey Millward

BLUE SKIES RESEARCH

When it came to you I
could never quite understand
how tangibility worked,
and you always had me
just as you wanted me:
blue skies research
in the sense that
you never set out
with the intentions of
discovering how to rip
a girl to pieces.

Morever:

I've gone two full days
without thinking of you
wholly, consciously –
two full days and to you
that might not seem much
but I'm breaking my back
trying to get people to
understand that god
damn, this is an
achievement.

This is an achievement.

Elouise Rugg (14)

DON'T!

Don't misuse your powers as a teacher
And tell me what to do
Or accuse me of things I have not done
Or never even planned to do

Don't talk about me to others
Or try to ruin my reputation
I'll be more relaxed when I confide in my father and mother
And it will help me fight the aggravation

Don't keep following me everywhere
Go do something else
And when a new accusation comes to mind
Go pin it on someone else

Don't pick on me for no reason
Because if you think I get affected, I don't
I will achieve what I want in the very end
And you will be overthrown

You think you're making me feel down
Disallowing me to clarify incidents any longer
But in fact I feel nothing but calm and collected
Because that which doesn't kill me only makes me stronger

I am stronger than you thought I would be
I'm not like others who fall to your constant yelling
Don't act deceptive towards your fellow mates
Because when I tell the true story it will become bestselling.

Rawda Moussa (14)

UNTITLED

I'd laugh along with them
the pain held inside,
with no ears that listened
I silently cried.

At first I would question
the things they would say,
why was I the victim
again every day?

Sooner and quicker
their words became clear,
it was standing in front of me
as I looked in the mirror.

They wanted me gone
they wanted me dead,
I tried not to listen
but the thoughts stayed in my head.

I'd lost everything
with only pain as my friend,
on my arms I had written
I wanted life's end.

I was finally happy
an escape, I was free,
too late to be saved
they could no longer hurt me.

Ellie Boyle (13)

SCHOOL LIFE

Waking up at seven in the morning,
Looking out to see the blue dull sky,
And all I wish is to sleep once again.

But, I continue to put my uniform on,
Eat my healthy breakfast,
And do my morning routine.

Waiting at the bus stop,
For a minute and a half,
And there, I sit reading my books.

Entering school,
And lessons begin, French, maths, English and RE,
Oh no, another day of hard work again.

By lunchtime,
I'm so hungry and sleepy,
Just waiting for the day to end.

Getting home to more homework,
Work through the equations and writing stories too.
Does school life ever end?

Finally, I'm done,
It's time to text my friends,
And relax before to bed,

And then my school day is over,
Enough hard work today,
But tomorrow it all starts again.

Eevon Foo (13)

ARE YOU DONE YET?

Spike you down,
Push me downwards,
Say this and that!
Are *you* done yet?

Say I ain't worth it,
Say despite of this and that,
Say and embarrass me!
Are *you* done yet?

Call me in front of the crowd,
Ha, ha, what a laugh,
Honey, beat me down I'll get back up!
Are *you* done yet?

Say out loud,
I'm titanium I say,
A wrecking ball I play!
Are *you* done yet?

You are not only done!
You are well done!
I'm the one having the last laugh!
You are so done!

Zainab Eniola Mohammed (14)

VOID OF RHETORIC

I question my thoughts
And I overload my brain
I questioned my perception
And had to experience the same

I questioned my situation
And then drifted off in my dreams
I questioned my ideas
And noticed recurring themes

I questioned an us
But could only answer half the question
I questioned the truth
But that only led to confession

I questioned her love
And then I questioned mine
It wasn't a question at all
It was a feeling not a find

I questioned my emotions
Possibly the worst thing to do
I questioned reality
Ended up feeling blue

I questioned my questions
And then stopped, said a vow
Talking is the only cure
For confusion right about now.

Joshua O'Connor (15)

THE UNKNOWN

Secrets are dug up into holes of snow,
I will know when the rain comes and I wash your happiness away,
Yes, it was me. I made it hail that day.
Instead of snow, may it rain ash and steel,
May it reflect exactly how I feel.
The white ice falls through my hair,
As I lie in the middle of nowhere.
I look at the stars, beyond my haze,
I stare and wonder why they are so far away.
You see hope in the mere globs of gas atoms,
And I see everything which cannot happen.
This piercing cold/grey season,
Reflects my eyes filled with inner demons,
My silent words condense in the fog,
As I drag your sanity away with mine,
In this chaos I named a life.
The voices ran to me like an upcoming train,
Even in this winter, in this beautiful rain.
I am an outsider with a spiral brain.
And high above the cruel sanity in the clouds I lay,
Behind the black walls and burning water,
I see the impossibility; the hurt, the slaughter.
Such beauty of the winter night, so free,
Is not deserved by someone like me.
The darkness swells into black tears,
And it rains down mortal fears.
I search and find the lies you leave,
Like a devil under a Christmas tree.
Snow burns at my cheeks,
Instead of ash; instead of heat.
Of the fire and magic which burns and churns
A twisted curse lives within this cold,
Waiting for a day without an oath,
For the white cannot hide the dark sounds;
The burnt black that becomes of the house.

The flakes become the notes of a silent serenade,
That coo the sounds of fate.
Run from my storm as it brews,
Run nobody, for who could hurt someone like you?
Forever a mystery,
And I hide in paper history,
The frozen becomes my destiny.

Mahanoor Abbas

TWELVE AGAIN

Ah, the sheer innocence of being twelve
No real responsibilities (apart from the occasional nag!)
I loved being twelve. Do you know why?
I had no worries, well, apart from the odd thing or two.
I was free to do whatever I wanted . . .
Well, within reason.

Now I'm thirteen and the innocence is gone
Responsibilities come into play.
People keep saying, 'You're not a kid anymore.'
But I'm not a grown up either.

Forget growing up.
I want to grow down,
Twelve is where you have no expectations, responsibilities or other 'Important stuff'.

Being twelve is the best . . .
I wish I could be twelve again.

Mhairi Jessup (13)

IF ONLY (YOU ARE SO MUCH MORE)

If only you could see yourself the way I do
not broken beyond repair, not damaged,
not even flawed or cracked.
To me you are the first raindrop on a steamy day,
you are the electricity pulsing through me,
you are the drum beat in a crowded arena,
you are the tears rushing in my eyes,
the stars in the sky.
You are the first snow fall in December.
But most of all you are the selfless boy,
you are the one who stayed up to save me,
you are the only one who seems to care,
whose hug can make everything better.
You are the one who makes me giggle,
when my entire world is falling apart.
Remember, you are so much more than the boy covered in scars,
whose liver gave up decades ago.
You are more than the suicide attempts
and you are more than the hospital visits
and the irrational fears at 3am.
You are so much more than your illness
and you are so much more than you think.
And maybe one day, you'll see yourself as I see you:
Brilliant.

Emily Scriminger (16)

CONFUSION

I've been floating on the surface for so long,
But now I'm beginning to sink.
I'll be trapped underwater
But I'm already locked in my brain.

Cars have crumple zones,
And protection from breaking.
Inside I'm broken,
Outside I'm just holding together.

It's like a warzone,
Though some call it a bombsite.
Straining where reinforcements are,
Waiting for what will cause the explosion.

The pain hasn't gone,
It will never leave me,
Not yet anyway.
It's just waiting patiently in no-man's-land.

Nobody can tell what really goes on,
They don't believe it anyway.
Why should they?
Outside I'm holding it together.

I can't hold it for much longer,
Any longer and I won't make it,
Any longer and even miracles will be impossible.

Rebecca Cawthorn (16)

ADULTS ARE ANNOYING

Adults think they're clever,
No matter what children say.
Adults think their brains are better,
In basically every way.

Adults barely listen,
And they tell me what to do.
They all think we are so silly,
Whether we're sixteen or two!

Adults like balanced foods,
'You need protein; eat some meat!'
They don't understand not hungry,
So they make us over-eat!

Adults just don't trust us;
They think we'll do silly things.
That we'll copy celebrities,
When all they can do is sing.

Adults think they are wise,
'We've got plenty of wisdom!'
Adults think we don't understand,
We have imagination!

Adults do what they want,
Because they are all 'grown-ups!'
Adults can be so annoying,
But we love them very much.

So, adults are clever,
And they are silly and wise.
They can be really annoying,
And their backs of heads have eyes.

But, adults are quite good,
And they look after us well.
So we do really love adults,
But, shhh, please could you not tell?

Shaunagh McSweeney (13)

JUST SMILE

Sweaty palms
Clenched fists
It's never good to feel like this

A salty tear runs down my face
I wipe it away
And leave no trace

They say anything, knock me down
And leave me with nothing
But a frown

I hide it away to show I don't care
Pretend that they
Were never there

I'm sick and tired, it's been going on for a while
So I turn my frown
Into a smile!

Kelsey Woor (13)

TEENAGERS OUT THERE

I sit on my bed and think about the people who really care about me.
Dreaming away as I realise children my own age think like me.
Play with my friends, walking away thinking, *do they really care about me?*
Me and Jay walk all over the place, as he is my brother, my aim is to look after him.
Dark as colour black, walk through darkness and suddenly stop.
What is the point of life?
Thinking about my parents and that gives me a smile.
At least I know that someone cares about me, someone I can turn to.
Don't forget you've always got your parents and guardians and your family members to turn to.
You're not alone, you have more people to turn to than you can dream of.

Onkar Singh Sangha (13)

LOVE

I have got a feeling
That I want to share
With care and respect
That this feeling teaches me.

The feeling is . . .
Love is a soft cushion
That can be shared
And can be broken.

Love is a symbol to life
It is a passion
That is shared
And used by

It is a feeling
That everybody has
From Dad to Mum
That they share

People to animals
Share this little element with them
Because of feeling they get
And the passion

Everybody is special
But only love can express you
Love is an unforgettable feeling
That is given to everybody

Love is something
That we all use and give
To every single person
That we love

Love has meaning
Of respect, honour and likeness
It is used for several reasons
And also shared for different reasons

This feeling can be felt
By the special people
That we like or spent time with
Everybody is special

Sometimes life gives you hard times
But love always washes it away
And relieves you

Life is a symbol of love
That gives you happiness
As well as sadness

But we have friends
Friends are always with you
In hard or good times
But the most important thing is that
They have a certain amount of trust.

Saumya Nath (13)

TEENAGERS, INNIT? (THE STEREOTYPE – A RAP)

There's a stereotype for us teenagers
Yeah, we're one and all the same
We all get up to no good and drive our parents insane.
We're all really moody and full of attitude
There's not a single word that leaves our mouths that isn't frankly rude
We all skulk around in alleyways with nothing to do
And you should hear the things we talk about, oh yeah, I'm telling you!
If we're not starting riots, then we're stealing stuff
And if you ever try to stop us then that's when it gets rough
We're always causing trouble, we're always bringing shame
And we don't even care 'cause to us it's all a game
'Cause we're teenagers, aren't we? We're one and all the same
We all get up to no good and drive our parents insane.

Anisha Morally (14)

THE RISING LEGACY OF ALICE

When Alice went home, and the songs were sung,
'Twas the night before Christmas and the rising sun,
For two brothers awoke, the tale would be told, to find not all was right,
In their cosy little home.

For Tweedle Dee and his brother Dum, the adventure was yet to end,
And a trip in to our world, the duo would descend.
To bring Alice back, so they myth often goes, and crowns her in place on Wonderland's throne.

With Hatter as guide and dormouse in suit,
The caterpillar waving them off with his bongo flute.

And through dangers untold, and hardships un-numbered, the team fought to survive,
This unlikely band of heroes made it out alive.

And in to our world, where we seemed to deranged,
They set off in secret, no desire to be slain.

Arriving at a house far greater in size,
Our beautiful wanderers knew they arrived.

One knock, two knocks, getting worried on three,
The door finally opened and shattered their dreams.

For in place of the gold covered walls and design,
The rooms were covered in dirt, reeds and grime.

When a gardener passed and came to the group,
He sat them down with a smile, and re-told what he knew.

For many years ago, when his grandmother lived,
The house was alive with music, wonder and a gift.

Of stories far greater than any child could dream,
Of a little girl down a rabbit hole, his grandmother often beamed.

And when people travelled from miles around,
She would entertain them with tales of merry-go-rounds.

Of Hatters and dormice and two bizarre twins,
The girl's tales would end just as sad as they begin.

With her leaving a place she soon called her home,
But with friends so precious, she could set them out in stone.

When asked what happened, the Hatter would soon hear,
That one day her friends would come and set her spirit free.

Asking her name, the twins' last hope was lost, as little girl Alice was long since gone,
No queen she will be, no dancing, no glee,
Their beautiful little friend lived to be one hundred and three.

With six children of her own, seven grand and eight great,
She kept the story living on, and never let it fade.

Looking over her shoulder, Dormouse was shocked to see,
Their little girl Alice, but barely a breeze,
Waving one last time, no longer small and shy,
She turned to a window and set off to fly.

A world of wonders we face in our dreams,
But for Alice and our friends, it's always better to believe.

Emily-Jane Vass (17)

LYING IN THE DARK

Sleeping in my room alone tonight,
fighting all my demons in sight.
Mama said, 'Close your eyes and shut them tight.'
This is all in my head, myths and legends don't exist.

I'm fighting my demons whilst you're asleep,
filled with happy thoughts and sweet dreams.
This is my war, this is my battle.

Tomorrow is another day I live to conquer,
the demons I've created in my head to fright.
They're striking again. Goodbye, goodnight.
No wait, what am I thinking?
I'm not ready for this.
This time you win, I have to, I need to turn on the lights.

Imani Lorrington-White (17)

FOREVER

The memories light up in my mind like a battlefield,
Each photo like an individual bomb
Exploding before my eyes,
Daring me to remember,
Daring me to question,
Daring me to think
About what really happened that day.

My brain is like a time bomb,
Each piece hard wired for something special,
So why can't I remember
The little things that once made me me?

All I know is what other people have told me,
That I was brave, and strong, and free,
But what use are other people's memories,
When what they tell me I can't even see?

My mind is a jumble of words,
Of sounds, of lines and blurs,
Trying urgently to make it all fit together,
But nothing ever seems to make sense.

Why must this life be so hard?
Like a never-ending road of hurt,
Threatening with every step you walk,
To swallow you deep under the dirt.

The only thing I can remember is what I saw earlier that day,
Before my train of thought went off down a never-ending track,
Promising me silently,
And secretly,
And violently,
That it would never return or come back.

I beg and plead and pray,
That one day you will find me once again,
My love, my sweetheart, my friend,
If only I could have asked you to stay.

But that is as much as I can remember,
The last thing I saw before it all went dark,
Your flawless face so full of sorrow,
Forever in my mind leaving a mark,
Forever being the promise of tomorrow.

Thea Watts (16)

UNTITLED

Sombre paradise
I feel like I am dying,
But everyone keeps lying,
They say that I'll be fine,
And that maybe, I just need some time

My cries fell on deaf ears,
No one understood my fears,
And now you'll be in tears,
The little girl you all knew well,
Is all alone in hell

While she wrote our letters,
You sat there and told her life would get better,
But that wasn't the way,
And today was her last day,
They tell the story of how they lost one life,
All in the hands of a silly little knife.

Shannon McGillian (15)

DISREGARD

I'm a potato chip in a crisp packet.
Yes I'm small, I'm not white, yellow nor brown.
No I do not taste plain nor am I covered in salt.
I'm surrounded by round plain potato chips,
which somehow all seem to represent each other.
They are just the same old boring chips . . .
But there's something strange, I'm not like the rest.
I'm not round, nor plain, I stand out, I light up this potato bag.
I'm somewhat special I guess.

You never know what to expect with these
creatures that dip their large, wide fingers into our
delicious potato chip packet. Sometimes
they love to stand and munch on our delicate
salty skin whereas at other times they want to
chew us up and spit us out . . . sadly due to the lack
of 'flavour' we produce.
I'm softer compared to the other potato chips.
I hurt, I cry, I see more compared to the others.
I've been pampered, I've been catered for but
I've also been stepped on, and spoken to in ways
one cannot imagine. I've been hurt sincerely due
to the lack of disregard and do you know what
they turn around to tell me?

'You're just a potato chip.'
And I whisper to myself, 'Ouch . . . you're cold.'

Natalie Attah (16)

UNTITLED

The roses were blooming
In the evening light
For a short while
My world was bright

Although it wasn't perfect
It was happy and warm
But soon my world
Tumbled into a storm

After a while
Roses began to die
Leaving my world
Torn apart inside

The roses were wilting
The violets were dead
My world was dark
And so was my head

My mind is corrupted
My feelings are torn
Leaving me broken
And barely adorn

It makes me feel sad seeing people this way
I don't want to have to just sit here and wait
Because by then it may be too late
We'll lose someone to their inevitable fate. Someone special.
The teenage years can be dark.

But it doesn't have to be . . .

Sarah Yule (15)

ON MY STREET

On my street night or day
Is the constant sound of careless cars and motorbikes rushing by recklessly,
The frequent sound of busses stopping breaks the deep silence of the night,
You can hear the sound of branches waving violently in the cold winter breeze,
Bash, bash,
The sound of the branches beating against each other starts to fade,
The leaves simultaneously fall to the ground
Like the beads of a necklace falling one by one
The whistle in the swirling wind haunts the neighbourhood streets,
Soon the sound of morning rain pelting against the dull cracked pavements echoes within the whole estate,
Soon the sound of school kids start to emerge
Like a hawk they screech,
Then there's the ones that moan and groan,
'It's too early!'

Above my street is a dark, angry sky,
With a huge blanket of smoke for clouds,
Green fuzzy moss grows on the walls,
Like a spreading rash it comes and never goes,
The blinding fog engulfs the air
Consuming every little bit of sunlight left in the sky,
The surviving leaves flop after a harsh beating in the wind,
Spiralling to the ground is a dry, crisp leaf,
It joins the pile of dead leaves scattered across the ground,
The tired, gloomy caretaker arrives
With his dirty old broom with worn out bristles.
He groans and yawns then looks at his watch,
'Another long day of work I've got.'

The smell of fresh rain and damp soil runs through the air
Pieces of cracked glass lie on the ground
From an old drunkard's late night row.

The brittle walls tower over you, intimidating,
Making you feel like a tiny ant,
The fresh wet grass lies in the sunlight
Whilst the morning frost melts and runs down each blade of grass
My street is not 'perfect'
But it is unique in its own special way.

Shabnoor Ali (15)

T.E.E.N.A.G.E.R

I don't like the way people look at me
I don't like the way people judge me
If you want something, come and say it to my face,
Hello, I am a teenager.

I'm grumpy and sad and miserable,
Nothing changes at all
I go to school, to study (that's what my parents think)
But all I do is text, LOL!

I'm not one of the good ones
Society explains it very well indeed,
We are thieves and criminals
We never dare to please.

So here's me right
A common teen you see
This is my explanation so far
About a t.e.e.n.a.g.e.r.

Kimberley Kisimbo (16)

I'LL MISS YOU ALWAYS . . .

(In memory of my beloved Komal Khala)

I think about her every day
And every single night,
I thought I saw her lovely face
And nearly shrieked with delight

I close my eyes wiping a tear
While wishing she was still here,
I'll hold the memories inside my heart
So that she is always near!

I thought I felt her touch today
In the breeze that passed by,
Then I remembered that tragic day
When I couldn't even say goodbye!

I thought that I would miss her
And never find my way
And then I heard the angel say
'She is with you every day'.

Vareesha Nasib (13)

SELF DESTRUCT

The lights are on but nobody is home,
Your soul is hurt, the monsters can roam.
Shut your eyes to hide from the world
Beyond our help, that poor baby girl.

Alone in the darkness like nothing will matter,
Starvation and purging but still getting fatter,
Dreams of your future dimming like fire,
With each accusation, attention-seeking liar.

Generations of youngsters, dropping like flies,
Maybe they'll understand when another one dies,
Judged by the world but they're not in your head,
Your hatred grows stronger with each word that is said.

Our children and parents, siblings and friends,
Are suffering inside, their pain never ends.
A cry for some help but no one replies,
Another cut in their skin, to hide from your eyes.

A night will come to end this hellish ride,
With pills in your hand or a gun by your side,
Too late for you now, no time for regret,
The happier future that will never be met.

Sophie Sweetlove (16)

TRUE LOVE

As the sun sets
I think of you,
The love that blossoms
Like candlelight
Flickering in the wind.

I think of you
As the stars come into place,
A hill and the stars,
For you and I a perfect place.

I think of you
Every second of the day
As love grows stronger
It feels unbearable now
Like steel holding a bridge
Nobody can knock it down

I think of you
Holding me, in the moonlight,
As we talk all night
With the bright twinkling stars
In our sight

I can say one thing
True love is what they say it is
Perfect in every way.

Amber Darby-Lunn (15)

INSIDE ME

The laces you used to tie your shoes in a pretty bow to take your first steps,
Hang round your neck, just as you're about to take your last.
The darkness crept up on you, just like you crept up on me
and captured my heart, and smothered it with every essence you owned.
I know you feel cold, but to me you're warmer than the sun's rays ever could be.
No one more than you deserves to let the light leak out.
But not to attract moths, but to draw in the butterflies and catch one.
You are a crispy morning on the start of May,
with dew jewels on the grass and baby birds learning,
spreading their wings for the first time.
I know you won't believe how beautiful you are.
You don't see the times when your forehead's a little wrinkled,
when your tongue pokes out as you concentrate on a test,
or when you're complimented by someone you love,
and it truly touches your heart,
so the blood rushes to your face, causing you to blush.
You don't see these things, and you never will.
You see your reflection, just a mirror.
Never you. And maybe that's just like the butterflies you wish to catch;
They do not ever see their beauty as the sun catches their wings
so precisely it shows they are carefully decorated.
Even when they land they don't let anyone too close to their
fragile frame, in fear of a simple touch.
You're delicate, but I won't break you.

Chanée Jae Holden (16)

BROKEN HEART

When I go away from you,
A ghastly glow comes upon my face
I try to go slow but the whole world quickens before I race
Each and every step I take
Each and every heart I break
My whole world shatters in smithereens
I try to entertain myself but it's no use
I think of you,
I love you.

Aiyesha Kaur Swarnn (12)

UNTITLED

Although you may think he is gone,
He is not.
His spirit lives on in secret,
In joy and happiness as he will.

There were many things he liked to do,
Many things in which brought him joy.
All beings seek happiness,
Happiness he sleeked.

He will carry the sky on his back,
As he watches over us,
Cheerful as he will.

I will never forget you,
Granddad Fred
Oh how I'll never forget you so.

Scarlet Victoria Paige Anderson (16)

THE LAKE

The lake so calm and still,
Water inviting you in,
Gentle caressing waves,
Warm summer water.
The lake deep and endless,
The water so tempting,
Rough razor like waves.
Still they ignore the warning,
The alarms in their heads,
And they jump,
Not thinking of their families,
Who cry themselves to sleep,
Their best friend who won't leave their room,
Their boyfriend who stopped eating,
Their loved ones just stopped living,
They just go through the motions,
But watch the door,
Half hoping,
Half praying,
You walk through the door,
But you don't,
You can't,
You're lying in a watery grave,
Until they decide to search the lake.
The watery body that holds,
Holds so many memories,
Takes so many lives,
Yet looks innocent enough,
And lives a lie.

Madeleine Peacock

MY SCHOOL DAY

My blaring alarm wakes me up, feeling dizzy,
I peel open my eyes, my hair looking frizzy.
I stretch and yawn and crawl out of bed,
Dreading this long-winded day up ahead.
I pad to the bathroom and what do I see?
My awful reflection staring at me!
I hop in the shower and tip back my head,
Wishing that I was back in my bed.

I trot downstairs to find some grub,
And pour some coffee into my favourite mug.
Then grabbing some bread, I shove it under the grill,
Burning my hand with the most ultimate skill.
After a few minutes what do I see?
My burnt toast smiling slyly at me!
I grab the charcoal lump, and shove it into the hole in my head,
Wishing that I was back in my bed.

I then retreat back up the stairs,
To try and fix my very messy hair.
I flip my head over and scrunch it into a bun,
Pushing in the bobby pins one by one.
Then I flip my head up and what do I see?
A bird's nest on my head, does it suit me?
I remove the nest from perching on my head,
Wishing that I was back in my bed.

Slopping back down the stairs I sling my bag over my shoulder,
What's in this thing, ten tons of boulders?
As I slowly walk out of the house,
I feel as confident as a little brown mouse.
Then I looked up and what do I see?
A gang of boys walking ahead of me!
I sigh and I shove my earphones into my head,
Wishing that I was back in my bed.

I get to school drenched in the cold,
My coat wrapped around me, like tight plastic mould.
In a huff I scurry down the hallway,
Pushing my way through each and every doorway.

When I finally get to my classroom, what do I see?
Everyone's sat at their desk, apart from me!
I walk in turning on my brain in my head,
Wishing that I was back in my bed.

Maths, History and French,
Make me want to jump into a world war trench.
But I don't, I sit down politely and say,
This day can't get much worse anyway.
So I look up from my book and what do I see?
Hundreds of equations staring at me!
So I slump over my desk and clamp my head,
Wishing that I was back in my bed.

I eventually get back from school, that almighty bore,
But I have homework, whose idea was it to give us more?
So I begin to scribble on paper,
Writing about science and some sort of vapour.
My eyes look to the clock and what do I see?
It's quite late it's bedtime for me!
So I finish my homework, my brain rattling in my head,
Wishing that I was back in my bed.

I crawl into my bedroom and slowly undress,
Finally feeling a little less stress.
I have returned to my duvets late at night,
So I quickly turn out the light.
I lay there in darkness and what do I see?
Nothing, and that's perfect for me!
So I close my eyes and rest my head,
I'm now safe, back home in my bed.

Amber Weyman (14)

IT'S IMPORTANT TO ME

I know it's important, but sometimes it's just too much,
The stress, the tension,
The uncontrollable apprehension,
It's just too much to bear,
How can I still be a kid, when they make us study?
English this, physics that and . . . 'Where art thou at?'
I know it's important, you tell me every day,
But sometimes I just want to relax and have a good play,
Is that too much to ask?

GCSEs are a pain in the bum,
I know they're 'imperative' but they're just not fun,
I want to study and get good marks,
But right now all I do is sleep and feel like I'm being bitten by glasses-
wearing-sharks,
Right now, it feels like the world is expecting too much,
But even so I have to put on a brave face and just go,
To school and back,
Study to 00.01 then sleep at quarter to raising of the sun,
I can't tell how much it kills,
To wake up one morning and find green around my gills,
I go to school and learn more stuff,
I know it's important, it's just too much.

Maleeha Mir (15)

UNTITLED

Violence isn't the way to fight the world,
Love isn't how to be happy.
Your face brightens on every positive
And it falls at every bad negative.
The way to travel through life happily
Is to follow your heart's motive,
And to motivate your heart
You need to let time pass.
Good things come to an end
But great things come to those who wait,
Lie down,
Close your eyes,
Imagination is the biggest surprise.
Nothing's too much, too big or small,
Make your ego bigger than all,
Because this is your only chance
To make something of yourself.
No one gets out this world alive.
When the world decides your fate
And time decides your peace,
You will drift happily away
Living the dream that you believe.

Eli-Louise Madden (15)

STARRY NIGHT

Twilight star, twilight star,
Shining high above so far,
Star light, star bright,
Will you grant my wish tonight?

As you shine above my head,
The patterns you show as I read.
Showing us your history,
Although it remains a mystery.

When I watch you as you fall,
Remembering that you were so tall,
As I watch you soar the land,
I look at those that still stand.

As I ran to catch your fire,
Asked my hearts true desire.
But then as I watched it flew,
Knowing that I really knew.

When I walked around that night,
Really seeing my home light.

Alessandra Birch (13)

GRANDAD I MISS YOU

Grandad I'll never forget all the stories you'd tell
Peach tins, salt shakers, fairies in a well
I'll never forget your useless knowledge and facts
Or that in summer you'd wear scarves and hats

Grandad I'll never forget when I'd come round for the day
You'd pick flowers for me, a rose for a rose you'd say
I'll never forget to learn ten words a week
After all a language is just what we speak

Grandad I'll never forget how proud you would get
Published poems, awards, medals French the top set
I'll never forget you just sitting in your chair
Or the cakes you would buy and then we would share

Grandad I'll never forget and I miss you each day
And I try not to get cross that God took you away
So I'm writing this about you so your memory can live on
I learnt so much from you grandad, you were the best,
I'm so sad that you're gone.

Grandad I'll never forget you . . .

Chloe Rushworth (13)

SONNET 155

What on earth is Christmas my darling, Beth
I enjoy the symbol that's out; the tree
Is the turkey done my master-classed chef?
Decorate it wavier than the sea.

What will I receive on the blessed day?
iPad, iPhone, iPod, what will I get?
It's against the law if I'm to dare say
Whatever you get you'll love it, I bet.

Grandpa and Grandma, will they come to stay?
They can stay in my room, it's warm in there
And if they come, I'll be able to play
Fine, but we'll have to ship their rocking chair.

Forgetful, are we? What does Christmas mean?
It's about the birth of Christ so it seems.

Anne-Marie Akinwale (13)

UNTITLED

Little Red Riding Hood is a story we all know
A girl with a red bag, I mean hood, or is it a bow?
Anyway Red had a task with a basket of treats
To walk through the forest and pass all the streets
The journey was dangerous and boy it was long
But Red thought nothing could go wrong.

Little Red Riding Hood basket in hand
A wolf's at the door now, it's just as he planned.
'Granny, I've brought you a basket of treats.'
'Come closer, Granddaughter if you'd like me to eat.'

I think that's how it ends, but I'm not really sure
Justice is served, though the story is obscure.
No one was hurt and the wolf went down
Red never walked alone, in that dangerous town.

Kelechi Otuonye (16)

THE GIRLS

When I walk into class,
The girls start to laugh,
They tell me I am nothing,
That I should go and starve,
I feel as if I am empty inside,
As if there is no way out,
I wish I didn't care,
But their words are so hurtful,
I wish I could stand up,
But I'm nowhere near that dare-ful.

They pull my hair,
They call me names,
I've got this new friend called a blade,
It makes me forget the pain they give me,
I get these thoughts into my head,
They are telling me it is the end,
I am just wishing it was all pretend.

They used to say, 'Hey best friend,'
I wish that had never ended,
But now they hate me,
What did I do?
I acted like good friends are supposed to do,
They didn't like the way I looked,
So I had to get a new look,
They called me vile and said I didn't have any style.

These girls just don't know when to quit,
I just wish they would 'rein in a bit',
I want to move on with my life,
Because I am beginning to see the light,
True friends I know will come along,
There is a way out that I see,
Things are beginning to look up for me.

Tamar Melton (13)

LOVE

Love is a game of war and hate,
Sometimes it's bad and other times it's great.

But what is the real point of love?
Is it a curse or a gift from above?

Like a roller coaster with ups and downs,
I see many grins but also many frowns.

People holding hands and kissing in the rain,
Others cuddling close on a London train.

Roses as gifts, the colour red so bright,
Staring at the stars in the moonlit night.

Valentine's Day brings cards and hearts galore,
Forgetful husbands rushing to the store.

Then follows the bad side, the side that we all view,
Arguing and shouting you hear quite a few.

Attempting to make up with chocolates and cake,
Or a romantic meal with wine and steak.

We are now getting distracted from this meaningful song,
Some relationships short but others can be long.

Then follows the wedding with a beautiful ring,
Family all together as the bells begin to sing.

Together forever is this a lie?
People splitting up makes us question why.

Getting a divorce and having to move,
The caring grandparents clearly disapprove.

Children at different houses every weekend,
Hoping and praying that soon this will end.

Unsure who are their real parents and which ones are fake,
Thinking it's their fault when clearly it's the parents' mistake.

The moral of this poem is relationships don't always last,
So try not to rush into things and don't go too fast.

So I ask again what is the real point of love?
It is a curse or a gift from above?

Lily-Jade Bartholomew (13)

UNTITLED

Some think that we are never right,
Some think we just like to get into fights,
Most think that we love running the night,
But that's just a teenage stereotype.

Some think we all hate to be in the light,
Some think that we are full of spite,
Most think that we are a dreadful sight,
But that's just a teenage stereotype.

We don't all start to moan and gripe,
We actually can be very polite?
So what's the reason for all the hype?
This crude teenage stereotype.

We don't want you to treat us just like knights,
And we're not saying that it's our birthright,
But it would be a true delight,
If you could abolish this stereotype.

Saundarya Mitter (14)

DRUGS

I watched her slip through my fingers when I got to the gate.
She ran, but I didn't chase.
That can't be love can it?

I step on the roller coaster,
There is no turning back now.
We go high; then we go low.
I can't stop, the ride is addictive.
I go on every time for the highest point.
When I get to the ground,
I have to go again!

It makes me so happy,
I keep on doing it.
The mental effects are great,
But the physical aren't so much.
My hands are turning black,
My teeth are rotting from the candy.

Nothing is the same anymore,
I thought the fair was cool!
I thought I was a man!
But I now realise,
I am nothing but a coward!

My life is slipping away every time I get on the ride,
But I can't stop.
I wish I hadn't started!
Don't start it ruins your life.
Don't waste your life and money.
You're better than that!
Go, go, go! Live your lives, don't wreck them.
You have more going for you than you think!

Kate Louise Young (13)

A MOTHER

A mother is like a flower,
a rose to be exact.
Or maybe like a brand new gate
that never comes unlatched.
A mother is like an owl,
both beautiful and wise.
Or perhaps a mother is like a ghost
whose spirit never dies.
A mum is like a heart that goes
strong until the end.
Where would we be in this world
if we didn't have a mother that would teach us right and wrong
and give us the hope and courage on what we need to succeed on today?

Halima Karbhari (14)

LIFE ISN'T FAIR

Parents complaining, homework that's due,
Confusing schoolwork; I don't have a clue!
But as I've sat down here, to rant and to rave,
I've realised: mine is a life that many would crave.
Children are hungry, yet I moan about lunch,
Some would die for my apple, yet I won't take a crunch.
Kids drink dirty water, yet I say I want Coke,
Others are dying, while I'll crack a bad joke.
And what do we do as this cruel world drags by?
We sit, and we moan, when we don't like our pie.

Jessica Campion (14)

VOICES

'You see my love,
it's because I care,' he said,
the malicious shoves,
from the stairs to the bed.
'Don't be frigid or scared,
just get undressed,
come on now,
do your best.'
Stripped of your poise,
and all you had left
you gave up your ploys,
and your efforts to be deft.
Sorrow lies within,
guilt swallows you whole,
as you touch skin to skin,
numbing your soul.
Lying battered and bruised,
you bled and you bled,
you know you're abused,
but he's already fled.
You clean yourself up,
no one will know,
grab a full cup,
and swallow your woe.
Everyone's dancing,
having a great time,
you spy a few glancing,
and catch a few mimes.

But now it's been a while,
and you're feeling okay,
you can even mange a smile,
from the odd day to day.
It wasn't your fault,
but you still wonder why,
he didn't think to halt,
when he saw you cry.
You pass him on the street,
and pluck up your nerve,

'What caused that feat?'
as you feel your spine curve.
You wait for a reply,
your blood filled with dread,
you look in his eyes,
'The voices; they said.'

Sophie Hamilton-Walker (15)

MUM

She winds me up,
She makes me mad,
I want to cry,
She makes me sad.

Sometimes I hate her,
And she hates me,
It's a natural part,
Of our family.

I wish she'd give me some freedom,
Let me clear my head,
Instead we carry on arguing,
But I end up in bed.

She really winds me up,
And makes me mad,
Because she's my mum,
And I am glad.

Brianna Mitchell (13)

UNTITLED

I feel I am owed, more than price or prejudice could wager
As it isn't pain I feel, or a known keenness for danger.
It's a repellent, some form of covetousness about me,
Which they all labour avidly to unearth.

Presumptions form like daggers pinning me to a post
The pins become aloof and they become engrossed.
But they cannot know of the pain ensued
Inside this incapacitated damaged body of mine.

All but nought wonder how it feels and ponder
How I uphold my pride, my body, how I wander,
But do not know the pain of your own reflection belittling
And mocking the person you used to be.

Unaware of my crowbar ribs, my threadbare fingers,
The pain which encompasses me, the pain which lingers
As if the spherical miracle gyrates on an axis of her own,
Leaving me behind and insubstantial and precarious and delicate.

Seeping like blood, my thoughts percolating sweetly,
To combat this body of mine which twists so completely
The struts that bind and hold said corpse together are crumbling, decaying
And I'll be gone, metaphysically so,
I'm sorry
For being
The way
I am.

Megan Dakers (16)

EVERY CHILD DESERVES TO SMILE

A girl, a boy, a damaged eye,
A broken future – a tragic lie.
These two children sit and wait; hoping for money, till it's late,
Beg all night and beg all day, it's their only option, their only way.
But it's not just three, it's not just four – it's hundreds, thousands and more!

To create a future you need a friend; to create a future we all depend;
Depend on love,
Depend on cafe,
Gain a sense of knowledge, with clothes to wear.

A city in India;
Not big, not small,
Holds an orphanage, out on call,
Takes in children who need that hope,
To help them through, to help them cope.
Learn to read, learn to write, learn to sing and live without fright.

Today I hope that we all donate, though not just with money, just to help create –
Create a smile by learning more, create a smile by making sure,
That you're aware of what I want to do – and that you become aware we can make a dream come true!

So today let's hold in the light . . . The children who have had to live fight,
Or, perhaps lost their loved ones – who are no longer in sight.

Let us cherish those who work, amongst the orphanage sensing change.
Every child deserves to smile, every day, all the while.
So let's support this working home, and come together so that they are no longer alone!

Shivani Daxini (15)

I CAN HEAR YOUR VOICE

As I looked up from the book, I saw them looking at me.
Why were they looking at me like that?
Their dark faces glared at me, judging my every move.
My eyes wandered the room, taking it all in.
The smell of nervous students mixed with the smell of whisky
A teacher would hide away, tickled my nose.
It wasn't the most pleasant smell, but it made me feel better,
More at home.
To my right sat that musty old cabinet.
I remembered it so clearly.
I ran my fingers across it and felt those same dents that were there last year.
But everything's changed since then
And I was certain no one would know the story behind those dents,
No one but me.
Why did this place always do this to me?
I can't let it take over my mind.
I decided to walk over to the window and instantly felt a sense of peace.
Whilst looking out, I saw the birds flying across the sky seamlessly,
Enjoying every move they made.
I wished I could feel that way.
Feeling a sense of harmony is all I've ever wanted.

My eyes decided to wander off again.
This time a poster attracted me. I've never noticed it before.
It must have been recently added to the room.
It made no sense to have a poster which read:
'If you ever need to . . . '
'No you mustn't read on. You just can't.
It wouldn't be right,' whispered an eerie voice.
I couldn't understand why this room would need to have a poster like that.
As I looked again, I saw a few faces looking at me as if I was some sort of disease.
I stared into the deep blue eyes of despair, reading her soul.
'I wonder why I decided to come to school today;
I knew I'd have to work with this weirdo again.'
I heard her voice clearly, but her mouth wasn't moving at all.

Then I remembered why it was occurring.
I always tried to block out what was happening, a way to forget that dreadful night,
But it always comes rushing back as if it is the reason for how I am today.
The gore, blood and the screaming, I still remembered it vividly.
Right in that spot, that corner is where they hit him;
Hit him until he couldn't scream anymore.
It's the sole reason I'm the way that I am today.
I began to consider following the advice on that poster.
Maybe I should ring them? No I can't. Why should I?
No one helped us when we needed their help the most,
How can they help now?
But maybe it could help me a lot.
I do need help.
Actually, no I don't. I don't need anyone or anything.
I took a few seconds to calm myself down.
I simply wished to be alone and free, just as those birds I had seen earlier.
Maybe if I just disappeared, no one would notice,
Just as that pathetic excuse of a dad never did.
Another bunch of days, I remembered clearly.
I couldn't understand why I was remembering all this
But there was a reason for me still being here today.

Iqra Arshad (17)

STOP READING A SCALE!

The only thing you look at is my weight.
How dare you judge me and determine my fate?
I do not starve myself, I am not anorexic.
No, you don't care . . . compared me a stick.
I am sick of these stupid assumptions!
You have no right to make presumptions.
Why do photos make thin girls sound ugly?
Apparently girls want to look like this in society.

Well, it doesn't look that way to me.
I look at blogs and all I see
Are people calling thin girls disgusting,
I have no words to describe how infuriating
This makes me feel.
Bounded by a seal.
A seal reading, 'Boys don't go for bone'.
This makes me feel incredibly alone.

I have cried endless tears,
I have unimaginable fears.
You say girls with a thigh gap are fake,
You say it like it makes you sick.
So you make curvier girls feel good,
But what about the thin girl who stays stood?
Standing, waiting for neglect?
Was making me feel ugly your intent?

Go eat some more,
Maybe it'll help you grow.
What do you even eat?
You look like you need a seat.
Why are you not hungry?
Maybe you shouldn't hurry.
You're so flat,
Ew you idiot.
You're like an ironing board,
They say as they gloat.

You should never judge anyone,
Until you know someone –

Only then will you figure out,
What they are truly about.
I hope you realise that thin girls are bullied as well;
I feel just as much pain, you may not be able to tell.
The word curvy sounds better than thin;
Thin sounds like it deserves to be in the bin.

I never call anyone fat or skinny,
Or bully someone if they are tall or mini.
Now you've heard things from my perspective,
I hope you realise that rumours are deceptive.
If you have more fat or less fat,
Always remember that;
The number on the scale
Is just a single detail.
This does not define who you are as a person,
This is something I know for certain.

Are the thoughts about your weight similar to mine?
Just remember that, it would make society feel sublime,
If your weight made you upset,
So do not feel regret.

You owe me nothing,
You can make something
Of your life. So try and strive,
To keep your spirit alive.

Maya Mahmood (15)

IT'S TOO LATE

She started high school,
With them saying she wasn't good enough,
Stories told,
Rumours spread
And she somehow heard them,
Then the social network came
And it got so much worse,
Telling her to just give up,
So she listened to the words.

How do you feel now she's gone,
And her family is torn?
How do you feel now she's watching you live on?
How do you feel now she's gone?
Think of what she would have done with her life,
You can cry,
You can hide,
You can flee,
But you're not innocent.

She started with a razor,
When she was shaving her legs,
Then it got to a knife,
When she wasn't with her parent,
Always wearing jumpers
To conceal her suicide attempts
And then they pushed her too far,
That she went over the edge.

Maybe next time you won't let it get that far,
Shut your mouth because
You know what the consequences are,
It's blood on your hands,
I hope you realise now,
You killed her yourself,

I hope you figured that out,
It's too late,
It's too late,
It's too late.

Nifemi Wilson-Adu (13)

UNTITLED

I had always imagined it would change, if I strived for what I hoped to always aspire to be.
I believed if I forced myself into a being I had always dreamed of –
one day my reflection would ensure me.

I've always wanted more than what the silhouette staring back appears to be.
And yes you can call me selfish, but these selfish traits are only what the world has persuaded me to see.

Unhappiness calls for one solution, you and me knowledge that however in my solving I feel nothing but grief.

What I once thought would have perceived my success, has actually forced and pushed me down an uneven road.

That reflection I ventured to see?

The one I always wanted to be?

It's still hidden because despite being able to recite and praise that 'I made it' – I didn't.

Satisfaction does not yet run through my veins, only my never needing crave of being faultless.

Hollie Jessica Murray (15)

I WANT YOU

You are a shining star
You are ever so far
You are my heart
What beautiful art
You are a miracle
So adorable
My heart was incomplete
You made it beat
Every day, every hour, every minute
There is no imitate
Be mine
I want you to be mind
I will shine
I will always protect
Never neglect
Remember I will always love you
So take my hand and be mine
And shine.

Murrium Mahmood (15)

THIS IS US

I know that there's this unbreakable bond
And it's been a long time,
Since we sat side by side,
Playing games and chasing.

Sometimes I feel you've forgotten me,
Sometimes I fear those eyes,
But there's always one thing I'll feel
And that's the love I carry inside!

Jasmin Kandola (13)

THE STRUGGLE

Darkness invaded the nights,
Screams of pain flooded the air,
Tears of fear echoed throughout,
Millions dead,
Children unfed,
A mother and father are left separated,
Whilst looking for their child,
But she's decapitated.

They will not give up,
Till their last breath they will not give up,
Till the day they are free
And victory is in arm's reach.

Nazia Sultana (17)

UNTITLED

There it is again,
That fake smile,
The one I loathe so.

I'm sure most people would call you brave,
I'm sure they're right,
But maybe it's my inexperience
Or my childish mind,
But to me you look like a fool.

Courageous to me,
Would be to have a scowl or a glare
At least we'd know the truth,
But that's the thing,

Nobody tells the truth anymore.

Lydia Venn (16)

GENIE

I wish for destruction.
A destruction so immense that it shakes society,
and brings death to those that bide us to the law of inequality.
They preach equal rights as if it was ever an option.
There's a reason why our last breaths are taken
by petty ending like starvation or even thirst.
For centuries man have enslaved each other,
to reach the peak of greatness
and despite the 'abolition of slavery'
we are slaves of the greater order,
we are slaves of the government
and until every man is free we are all slaves.

I wish for universal blindness.
For our eyes are the roots of all selfish desire,
we love with our eyes, all things that we should want to earn.
Beauty, money, sex and even hatred.
All animalistic behaviour thrust upon our human nature,
comes from the inability to see and learn of something's value.
With our eyes we pass judgement, lie and cheat.
Our eyes suppress our hearts,
to the extent that we won't love because one doesn't attain beauty,
we won't like because one has insufficient funds,
and we won't help because what we see is what we get
and helping a drug addict is exactly that! Helping someone addicted to drugs.
Money and beauty play no part in the individual's recovery.

I wish for no wishes.
For being given such opportunities puts you in a place of deep thought
and with the demons of society hiding in my mind
I might end up wishing for peace and equality,
like such things could ever be possible.
My wishes would be wasted,
as peace would lead to war

and equality to inequality.
Remember! God made us in peace
and all equal.
Man created war and inequality.
No genie could change that.

Hena Bryan (17)

I WAS TOLD

Dark.
Blackness.
No sight, no sound.
As the brightness shatters
I fall to the ground.
Are you there? Are you calling?
Reach out, I can't see!
Fiery clouds are becoming
Too repugnant to breathe.
I can't breathe.
I can't see;
A malevolent phantom has hold of me.
She's a face of tears,
A heart made of rock,
A malign soul,
Her name is shock.

Nell O'Neill (14)

I HAVE NOTHING TO SAY ABOUT AUTUMN

(Dedicated to Eleanor, because this was all her idea.)

Don't they say,
When you have nothing to say,
Don't say anything at all.

I disagree,
But in a peculiar way,
When you have nothing to say,
Let the world speak for you.

Like today, of all days,
The green of the trees,
Slowly turns orange.

The air,
From warm summer breeze,
To brisk winter wind.

Cools my blood,
With pleasant fingers,
Of almost frost.

The swallow song,
Fades into the sky,
And the robin takes the stage.

The soft petalled flowers,
Shrink into the shadows
To give the holly light.

The sun becomes weary,
And the moon decides
To come out and play.

Dusty gloves and scarves
Are brought down from the attic
To warm, frosty fingers.

So, suffice to say,
Though I have nothing to say,
Autumn certainly does.

Holly Russell (15)

HAVING A DREAM

Having a dream is to push you forward,
Make you happy,
Make something of yourself,
No one should tell you it's impossible,
Because anything can happen if you just believe.

Having a dream is just fantastic,
In your imagination,
You're there,
If you try hard enough,
Your dream becomes a reality.

Having a dream is as wonderful as chocolate,
As imaginative as Roald Dahl,
Don't ever think, not once,
That it can't come true, because the truth is
That people who tell you that they are miserable,
They never dared to dream.

If you haven't dreamt of making something of yourself,
Then give it a thought,
What's the worst that could happen?
Inspirational people are all around us,
Famous idols didn't get there by just doing nothing,
Stand up for what you believe in and be true to yourself,
Then your dream will come true.

Even if that's not being famous,
Doing what you love is a dream come true,
Be an amazing person,
Be proud of yourself and the people most important to you,
Most importantly make a difference,
Then your dream is a reality.

Rhiannon Walsh (14)

TEENAGE LIFE IS WELL CONFUSING

Feeling young then feeling grown,
Sometimes my body doesn't feel like my own,
Adults don't listen, kids don't understand,
Someday I don't even know who the heck I am,
Mum says teens speak their own language,
I don't know what she means
My girls on Twitter know I'm totally 'reem'!
And OMG, why do parents try and act cool?
Weren't dinosaurs roaming when they were at school?
Heading to college, school was such a struggle,
Most of the time living in my own little bubble,
Now making new friends, basically starting again,
These teenage years never seem to end,
It's seeming like forever but time goes so fast,
Hopefully soon I'll be a grown-up at last,
Growing up stuff isn't so amusing,
Don't you know teenage life is well confusing!

Jazmine Randle (17)

FOLDING MY CARDS

Not being able to feel would be better than this endless pit of pain
I am currently cascading down into, falling further and further,
and never reaching the end of life where pure bliss of death awaits.
Forced to stay in a living hell on Earth
where all my fears and nightmares are brought alive.

Silver, reflecting moonlight from my hands.
It can bring me joy and end this tortuous production
that you may call life. Because that's all it is, a production,
a theatrical performance put on for the benefit of others.
Whether you get cast in a good part
is past our judgement and decisions.
But ending your role early is in the set of cards that you were dealt.

Gliding my escape and freedom across the naked armour
I begin to feel the red velvet pour from my empty shell
and feel it pool at my feet as I give into the darkness consuming me,
collapsing onto the ground my weak caging as delicate as ever;
I relish in the last few seconds of misery and suffering before flying free.

Genevieve García Hall (14)

BROKEN BOND

They think they know us, but they don't.
They try to understand us, but they can't.
We try to reason with them and we're lost.
We try to reach them and we fall,
But that's what makes us teens after all.

In life, we already begin before we start.
We're vulnerable; innocent in the heart,
And sometimes we fall apart.
We are adamant and insecure,
But for hope we are rest assured.

We are still the baby you held years ago.
The one you adored and worshipped all day long.
We haven't changed in heart, only in years,
We still yield for your warm embrace
And hope one day we will end this misperception.

Mary Aikhuele (14)

JUST WATER

Life is enjoyment as much as it is defeat.
It is also very much character as much as it is (arguably) aesthetics.
Sometimes people dismiss this statement.
They dismiss good character for the materialistic, spur-of-the-moment
pleasures of an aesthetically pleasing fantasy.
And why? Why do people insist on making an impact,
regardless of its resonance in another person's life?
I suppose they wouldn't like to watch the movement of water,
on a deserted beach somewhere where the sky is overcast;
they wouldn't be completely entranced by its simplistic motion,
nor with someone else's good character.
But rather, lust for the aesthetics of people who see no entrancing
simplistic motion, just water.
This is why the rarity of a mere good friend is,
in my opinion, a great flaw in our existence that has lasting impact.
The aforementioned dismissal creating lost, damaged and lonely people.

Niamh Honey (15)

TEENAGERS

My wrists are red,
They used to be blue,
My wrists are scarred,
Does it look good to you?

My hair is straw like,
It used to be brown,
It wasn't that good,
So I let it down.

My eyes are bloodshot,
They are colourless and dead,
But they were too small,
Now they're just red.

My body is thin,
I got what I want,
I was too fat,
But it's all gone wrong.

Emily Hirst (13)

THE BOY

Thank you dear Mother, for midnight black hair,
That merges with shadows that really don't care,
As I call them my brothers, my sisters, my home,
As I ride them throughout this city of stone.

Thank you dear Mother, for pretty blue eyes,
That glitter like ice and draw envious sighs.
And find swiftly the figures, as they try to escape,
And stare forward ahead, into dead mouths that gape.

Thank you dear stranger, for this beautiful life,
For the dancing of shadows and guns and my knife.
Thank you for showing me this world of insanity,
For me to be born with no sense of morality.

Thank you again, for the sun and the rain,
For a child's simplicity, and luck that's insane.
For giving death's power to this strange little creature.
Thank you.
So sorry I can't remember your features.

Liza Steinberg (16)

MY WORLD

A stylish touch and party theme,
Celebrity like and streets are clean.
All the gardens here are party venues,
With smiling dance floors and five star menus.
Red carpets rolling from your door to your road.
This world is a bullet on celebrity mode.
Delighted disco balls inserted in every room
Shimmering giant speakers placed in every town,
Blasting new tunes, they won't let you down.
Lonely lamp posts, no they don't exist here,
Instead we have spotlights to keep our roads clear.
The calm cars glow in the dark so fantastically bright,
The headlights get better, made of multicoloured light.
We can't forget the humble houses with the stylish mirrored bricks,
And the magicians who walk through towns with impressive magic tricks.
Not to mention every waterslide that beckons you
And funfairs full of crazy, excited, fast rides too.
My world is a wrapped up present, unknown, a surprise,
When the presents unwrapped no one will hide.

Megan Hassan (13)

MURDERER

There lives a murderer, Dave is his name.
People whisper, they say he's insane!
He's mad, scary and he's off his rocker
And he likes to drink chocolate mocha.

Clock strikes twelve, time has finally arrived,
A very evil spirit Dave has thrived.
Slowly creeps like a naughty school child,
Pounces on his prey like cats in the wild.

He hides amongst the shadows; owl in the dark,
His victim; dead, yet he has not a mark.
Back up the hill and into his house,
Sneaks very quietly, quiet as a mouse.

In the kitchen to pour a cup of tea,
Darkness outside is all that he can see.
All the way up the stairs, and into bed,
Falls into his dreams and rejoins the dead . . .

Ella Preece (13)

FATHER

To say I care would be to say
That I mind.
And I refuse to care for you,
An old pine.

Strength and power is in your roots.
And your leaves,
They carry signs of freedom lost
And of me.

When the storms rage and the wind
Gets you carried away,
You hit back and a bird
Cries out to make you stay.

Don't walk down that dark, cold road.
If it means that you will stay,
I will cut away at my imperfections
And pretend that your sadness is not contagious.
Till then, cool off and take a breath
And pray it's not your last.

Isabel Wauchope (17)

UNTITLED

The weather is hot
but my heart is left cold
for fear of the unknown is a fear of what's untold
for death is near
and dread is clear
but the glimmer of hope
and the thought of being free
is what pushes you
and helps you cope
to deal with fear
is to deal with your tears
to think ahead
and think of better
to forget that vendetta
and feel grateful instead
life is great
when you know you still have a chance
to redeem yourself
and be a better person.

Jake Brown (16)

WHY?

Why cause yourself pain?
Why make marks?
Why make tears, over some words?

You are strong
You are unique
If people don't like it
Well it's tough luck for them.

When you get down
Pick yourself up
Don't pick up that knife or compass
Is it really worth it?

The scars shall remain
For forever and a day
You are more likely to get picked on
For the faded purple marks over your arms and legs.

So next time someone hurts your emotions
Walk away and don't retaliate
Draw a picture
Or go for a walk
Just don't cause yourself pain or more purple marks.

Truda Koppelow (14)

COLD AND LONELY HEART

When you're not here, my heart longs for you
When you disappear, my heart stays strong for you
And when you're gone, and you took my tears too
My poor, helpless heart, beats only for you
When you were here, and the skies were no longer grey
You had to make me feel that there was no other way
But to give up my heart and soul
And when the blue skies were gone, it was no longer okay,
A flash of lightning – and it rained all day
The rain shan't stop – I doubt it ever will
But in this poem I write without thrill
My heart will forever and always stay true
Though you bashed it and smashed it black and blue
On a cold winter's night, I whisper and stutter
Your name, your name, I trudge through the gutter
My soul was yours, with which you took
Beat it over the head with a hard, stubborn book
Of love, not hate, and then I discover
I don't need you, I just need time to recover
From the pain you caused, and the agony too
And thus ends this tale – I shan't be waiting for you.

Beth Jones (13)

HE SITS ALONE

He sits alone,
Yet he doesn't know,
I sit beside him,
He sits alone,
We talk, we laugh,
He walks a lonely path,
I offer comfort not alone,
He sits alone,
I'm alone,
We all sit alone,
I'm gone,
I never was,
He sits alone.

Sophie Cutts (14)

A PINT OF BEN & JERRY'S

What is she? A medal to add to your talented collection?
Individually pathetic. Together impressive.
Did you work hard? Probably not.
Shameful to think someone could be so naive.
So blind she did not see reality, but a mirror to reflect her feelings.

Did you damage her? Definitely.
The cracks seen by her loved ones, her mirror and the bathroom scales.
The needle fluctuates and her confidence wears thin.

Do you care? Hopefully.
But more to the fact she understands.
As she watches Grease for the seventh time
She knows the beginning, middle and end.
Reciting the words to herself on the sofa with a pint of Ben & Jerry's.

Ellie Pickles (16)

A MOTHER LIKE YOU

You have always loved me since I was born.
You always told me from a little acorn
A might oak tree would grow.
No father. You were on your own.
You were selfless, caring, committed, devoted.
You played with me, cared for me and disciplined me.
I didn't understand, I didn't appreciate you
But now I do Mother, I do.
You always said I was blessed by God,
And I was naive enough to believe it –
It has taken sixteen years
And after all the tears
You still show mercy –
Now I truly see, God has blessed me, with a mother like you.

Ilona Makhunova (16)

MY FOREVER PLACE

I am light as a feather,
I am a nobody.
the urge to scream, to fight, to thrash
dies deep within me.

I am shattered
and broken,
but yet so peaceful. Harmony.
I give into the deep mystic lake.

I am limbless
my heart is staggering bright, white.
Is this it?
My forever place . . .

Tasmina Khatun (16)

SPOILT

As far as ditches dive
And where mud full paths collide,
A rich and sweet desire
Is what brings me on this ride?

Running free and humble
Replaces my anguish as I stumble,
A graze, a scratch, to be risked
To carry on and not crumble.

First I climb the rocky head,
Although this part I usually dread,
If the skies show me stormy rains
Then for me I go back to bed.

But if the skies do be true,
And all is well for this day too,
Then perhaps I'll venture on
And present my paradise, even to you.

Only I have been witness to this place
If everyone could find it they'd be here with haste,
But this is mine now, and so it should be
Hidden and protected, should be its case.

Special as it is, with exquisite blue shores
And unique wildlife never visited before,
Its once hidden secret is exposed to its neighbours
I suppose new invaders are expected of course.

But to this day, I wonder how
If there were places like this found
That could be saved from ailing visitors
How would we stop ourselves from keeping it bound?
Once discovered never the same around.

Sid Gillam (16)

A TEENAGE MIND

I don't want to leave it until it's too late,
When I'm wrinkled and old
And I don't leave the house because I'm afraid of the cold.
When I've forgotten what it's like to have teenage thoughts,
When I look back and realise that the things that I sought
Are long gone now; they slipped through the seams
And I've forgotten how it feels to have teenage dreams.
The world's a big place and I don't want to get lost,
But when there's a whole universe to explore I suppose that's the cost.
I know everybody goes a little mad sometimes,
I sit and I sit and I come up with rhymes
But how do I know I'm not wasting my time?

I drown myself in words to keep my head above the water,
And keep doing my best to be a good daughter,
Hoping one day real life will be like fiction,
That one day I won't be this walking contradiction.
Because there are still so many sunrises and so many sunsets,
And cities I've never been to, filled with people I've never met,
There are so many stories to hear and sights to see,
Kisses and laughs and books to read,
There doesn't seem to be enough hours in the day for the things I want to do,
The oceans I want to cross and the mountains I want to move,
The things I could be doing if I only got out of bed,
I am too many thoughts in too little head.

At first I thought I wanted to be a poet,
When really I think I just wanted to be a poem.
They tell you and tell you that 'you can do anything'
But the only thing I hear is that 'you have to be everything'.

Katie Mahon (15)

UNREALITY

'Half dreams, half reality,
a fond understanding of the insanity,
an endless confusion from the reality,
how can truth be so cruel and faithless?
When lies lovingly fill the void truth creates,
a tender blanket of false concepts,
to shield from the harshness of consciousness,
wrapped in the comforts of unreality,
cloaked in passiveness,
to preserve the fragments of a broken soul,
sound is stilled, the end is near,
the deep breath before the plunge,
is shattered into a million pieces by the light,
the merciless light,
it burns through the blanket of dreams,
it forces you to see,
but how beautiful can this one sight be,
your hand to pull me through the web of lies,
strong hands to put the pieces back together,
and set my soul in radiant fire,
I am content.'

Bridie Neale (16)

MY SPECIAL BEAUTIFUL

I may not have shiny smooth skin,
I haven't the big beady eyes,
And I'm not the perfect type of thin,
But I don't need attention from guys.

I may not be the prettiest,
I do not have long spiders' legs,
And my breasts are not the biggest,
But I don't care for turning heads.

I may not have long blonde fair hair,
I'm not the most fashionable,
And I don't care for what I wear,
I'm not fussed about the label.

I may not have expensive shoes,
I don't cake my face in make-up,
And I don't have a nice hair do,
But I don't want a cover-up.

With my tangly brown hair, and boring plain clothes,
Slanted smile, squinty eyes, and crooked nose,
I am so very different from the rest.
I do not set out to look the utmost best.
I am my own person, unique, individual,
I am my own special kind of beautiful.

Megan Jenkins (17)

THE THINGS I COULD NOT SAY

Should I write another poem about love?
Boy meets girl
And they live happily ever after.

Should I write a sonnet?
Fourteen lines long.
Ten syllables per line.

Or maybe a couplet?
The last word
of each line
rhyming
each time.

Will a flow of words
in an order
even
I
cannot
understand
be sufficient for you?

So many things
I want to say,
but not enough
words.
Words.
Words.

A poet
cannot even
put into words,
how
I
feel.

A thousand thoughts
I want to share
but cannot.
Rather,
to tell you

what I cannot say
is much easier.

I cannot tell you
that you are on my
mind
constantly.

That I want to
fall asleep
with your arms
wrapped tightly around me
listening to your heartbeat.

I want to know your
likes and dislikes,
your fears,
hopes and dreams.
And what you are thinking when
your eyes
glaze over.

And I completely
cannot
tell
you
that my heart
skips a beat
when you smile.

That I count the days
until I will
see you again.

And I could never let you know
just how much
I
really
like
you.

Aster Gordon (16)

DECEIVING EYES

It's like screaming as loud as you can
From inside a closed metal box
No one can hear. No one will care
They're fools to her laughing eyes

She has a smile that lights up the room
Yet inside she's shedding tears of sadness
Fearing people's judgement
Fearing her own madness
Her insecurities control her mind
Her millions of regrets and mistakes
These are things she designed.

She is known to be tough, fearless.
The personality that everyone envies
But a blade strikes her wrist at any opportunity.
This, nobody sees.

She's the girl with the contagious laugh
The lips that speak only nice words
Yet she is dying inside
Simply because of those deceiving eyes.

Priya Pri Mahalingam (17)

PACE

You're stuck, can't budge
In this hole you're in.
The pace you went was
So slow you fell in.

Now the life you know is
Stuck on repeat,
Like a battered old tape
From the noughties.

Your routine goes around
And around,
You wish something would
Turn upside down.

But the only thing you can
Do is wait,
Wait for the pace to pick
Up again.

You're only at the beginning,
There's still so far to go,
Just wait a while
And continue in slow-mo.

Gabriela Suarez (15)

THE SHADED GIRL WITH THE ANGEL WINGS

The shaded girl with the angel wings,
Laid and prayed for all of those disturbing things,
To escape from her devastated mine.

The tears of blood dripping from her eyes,
As they begin to figure out all of those dreadful lies,
That she kept hidden away for so long.

The dangerous bottle that should never be released,
Because by that time the fragile girl would be lying still on her bed deceased,
And soaring to the heavens for a safe escape.

As all of those terrifying memories return to eat her to the core,
She begs that one day she will soar,
To set free from this caving life.

Head held low she walks the town,
With all of her frightening feelings hauling her down,
To the presence of the Devil inside.

Heart of stone and soul of ice,
She longs for that hopeful roll of a blooded dice,
That will drag all of her terror away.

The shaded girl with the angel wings,
Hovers and wails as she sings,
About her indescribable experiences.

Bethany Tomlinson (15)

FREE

We embark on a long journey to free
our mind of all stresses,
to treasure and make
these moments last longer, forever.

I've had enough,
hounded by fear,
afraid to let go,
afraid to come near.

I swim in the deep ocean,
I inhale the pyroclastic flow,
I walk on the nettles,
and I thaw out on the snow.

I feel free,
lighter than air,
floating on clouds,
as buoyant as can be.
If this is a dream,
do not pinch me.

No rules.
No limits.
No boundaries.

Mahbuba Begum (18)

THE LIFE OF A TEENAGE GIRL

Online browsing of the latest fashion and trends,
Twizzling my hair and picking out split ends.
With late nights at the weekend, staying up online,
Spending my time on Facebook, although I'm short on time.

An early morning rise with the parting of my bed,
Time to wake up now to sort out my face and head.
First I sort out washing, then combing and shampoo,
Then I continue to make up, well I think this should do.

After I'm primped and primed, I venture to the outdoors,
But walking past the mirror, I spot my over-sized pores!
To others they seem minor, to me their existence clings,
Why you may ask, I'll never know, it just seems to be a thing.

Adults don't understand; things have changed since 'their day',
The more they boss us about, the more we will disobey.
'Act like a lady and sit up straight,' they shout,
I just want to have fun, what are all these orders about?

With pressure from the media, to be perfect in every way,
It's no wonder a girl stresses too much, every single day.
Our idols have perfect figures and are just generally flawless;
We want to be just like them, because we're overcautious.

But everyone has their flaws and their insecurities;
We seem to grow up fast, with strong maturity.
However, a teenage girl is still a child at heart,
A figure of which she will never leave or part.

Katie Myatt (14)

DUST OF THE APOCALYPSE

I'm new to this world,
Among the crowded faces
And patronising smiles and jingles,
I stare,
As the dust of the apocalypse rains down,
In town children will play in the cold,
Creating their white ash moulds
In acceptance of what has to be accepted.
As the dust of the apocalypse rains down,
Adults will find their wallets empty,
Yet the display windows still so tempting:
The war of shopping will begin.
You see, the bargains are what started it,
As bodies crush in the hope to get that one . . . thing,
All seems irrelevant really,
Especially since they all worship,
The red-faced obese man who seems frozen in the McDonald's window.
Coincidence?
I think not,
Since the dust of the apocalypse still rains down,
I have closed all my windows,
And stayed in a blanket bundle,
I will not get a looming Christmas tree,
As the dust of the apocalypse rains down,
No,
My friend I will sleep till the world's end,
And smile at human idiocy,
As the dust of the apocalypse rains down . . .

Milli Hylton (14)

WELCOME TO MY LIFE

(Dedicated to Amanda Todd)

The anger inside, locked up inside,
I won't allow out,
Because if I do I'm going to blow up,
The temptation to cut is an overwhelming feeling,
Soon enough it will be too much,
You make a mistake then try to make it right,
But nobody listens, all they want is a fight,
To make your life more miserable by the end of the night,
It's getting to the point where I just want to take flight,
I cry, cry, cry, moaning in endless pain,
I'm ashamed of the way my blood flows down the drain.

It's school the next morning, my personal hell,
The Devil would be proud of my language as well,
I stutter and I fumble, drop my books to the ground,
I watch the jocks use them as footballs not making a sound,
Stumble to my seat, listen to the unfamiliar creak,
Letting the monsters know I'm here.

Pain, pain everywhere, they caught me again,
I'm used to it now, but I have no defence,
I'm talking to a brick wall,
No one listens anymore,
My mistake cost my social life,
Will it cost more?
So many questions running through my head,
Every day, every night, asleep in my bed,
I'll never know what loving is,
But lately I don't really care,
The monsters are destroying me,
My emotions are leaving me rapidly,
One day I'll wake up but I just won't be there.

Aliesha Woollin (14)

GREENSLEEVES NO MORE

He once told me that I did wrong
to cast him off discourteously
for he claimed he loved me so
and delighted in my company.

He sang of my gown of green,
a king who admired the knights of old
both day and night sang to me,
that I was his heart of gold.

At my hand he granted what I
would crave;
at his games he wagered his life
and land –
yet he sent me to an early grave.

It seldom brought him joy to sing
of my gown of green,
alas! How long it has been
since he, my Lord and King
sang of my spirit once so free.

He prayed and prayed to God on high
that I, his lady, may be judged to die.
No more did green please him so;
and though I pledged mine own sweet love,
he let the blood of my body flow.

It seldom brought him joy to sing
of my gown of green,
alas! How long it has been
since he, my Lord and King
sang of my spirit once so free.
Once a lover in captivity
now he hath decreed my bloody
end to me.

Ashleigh Black (19)

FRIENDLY FIRE

Hope is lost, and you foster feelings of doubt. Out with it!
you say, the grenade you made for me
to pierce the fierce follicles
of faith flying towards my face – but wait!
The food for thought you thought you had
surprises you; arises, a glimmer of hope.
You shake, you're scared, I stare at the star
of your life, you, the protagonist and antagonist
of your own story. The glory
and promise of fame, turned to shame
when no one remembers your name
anymore because you blend in, fending for your identity
even so and you grow up
and down
and retreat from the battlefield. You wield
no weapon no more- no more!
You cry and I testify to the Lord that I don't believe in but do so for your sake
and say:

I believe in you more than the fictional friends
you made when you were eight,
when you said you wanted to be dead
and they said
it's okay to be scared. And you knew that they cared
and stood by you while the idle teachers preached
nonsensical keywords no one heard and then
let you get tormented because
life's unfair, apparently. You told me you can no longer see
your friends – they beat them out of you at the age of ten and then
they asked you why you looked so sad.
When you were eleven you were
a ghost already – post-breakdown, around
you looked through books and crooks and crannies
but all you found out
was that privileged kids of middle-class and higher
were liars
and the working class were supposed to look for the greener grass
even though the last sight you saw
was the sun running for cover behind a ton of

concrete, and a dust-bowl for weeds
who were just unfortunate flowers who came expecting more warmth
but found only
a face-full of frost.
You crawled into scrawled
words and heard nothing,
hibernating, hyperventilating and deoxygenating
and nobody was there to hear you scream.

You told me this five years later and I was shaken,
but making nothing of it,
taking nothing from it,
not realising I was the last lifeline
in your eyes and that your disguise was foolproof
and I was a fool, a fool to believe you were fine
because years of schooling assuring and obscuring
the hole that was boring its way into your heart; the art
of indoctrination, suffocating you without knowing anything. Destroying
you was my deepest regret, but getting
the answers to questions led to the revelation
that the chloroform-shawl that muffled you
had been mine once, too, and at once I understood.

I tell you this and brace myself and look down to see
that the pin was never pulled.

Juliette Hills (15)

QURAN

Quran, the holy book sent down for mankind
To cherish, enlighten and place peace in the heart and mind
For men and women, young and old
All around the world, the Quran is sold
The glorious Quran, the words of Allah
Sixty-seven times is the mention of the word Salah
Revealed to the prophet Muhammad over the course of twenty-three years
The stories of prophets, Sahaba and more, this is just a glimpse of what the Quran shares
Written in Arabic, from start to finish
The words so meaningful, it's a cure to all blemish
For those who memorise it by heart
They are the preservers and won't let it part
The book has stayed in its original form, without having been altered
The many Hafiz's including the prophet himself, he never faltered
The Quran, the book of life, shows us how to live from A to Z
You'll know it's a book of truth, reality and more, for those who have read
The true understanding makes us more aware
We know the day of resurrection is drawing near
It's time to act fast, time to make a change
Our lives need to be rearranged
This life's a test, the real one's coming soon revealing our true fate
So let's all amend our ways, before it's too late.

Marya Shamim (14)

ASYLUM

Here I sit in this asylum
My blood writing these words
My nails are torn and bloody
From dragging them down these walls

Here I sit in this asylum
Rocking back and forth
Wishing that these voices
Would silence their chorus

Here I sit in this asylum
Pounding at the door
Wishing that I could see the light
As the darkness clouds my soul

Here I sit in this asylum
Trapped inside my mind
I am forever imprisoned
And I can never get out.

Elise Miskelly (16)

OBLIVION

Something happened today
And I got lost in myself
I don't know where I am and I'm not sure I'm ready to know yet
But I feel a kick in the bottom of my gut
And it's telling me to stay in this world I've never seen
I'm scared because all I see is here in a space of isolation
I know this doesn't make sense and I don't expect it to
But there's something inside me, lurking in my sight every second
I'm pretty sure it's beautiful but I don't know why
I'm craving to know the answer because it's choking all reason
But I know as soon as a I drop my guard, I'm vulnerable to pain
Every damaged person says can ruin everything
If this is what I think is settling in my heart, then I will live in fear
As the most elegant feeling will either make me a better man
Or break me to oblivion.

Jackson Fenton (19)

INTERNAL INNOCENT

The wails of the night,
Startle anyone who hears,
And embraces us with a profound fright,
Freezing our blessed thoughts.

No one listens to the words,
We think only of the dangers,
Pitiful are the cries that are blurred,
And hidden behind the terror.

But if we silence the wails and cries,
While welcoming the meek voice,
There will be a small child with innocent eyes,
Paralysed in society's scorching grasp.

The nightmare that she speaks,
Is our greatest fear of all,
That we do not wish to seek,
The fear of being forgotten and alone.

Phoenix Rising (15)

THE BOY

He looks to the moon, all he does is stare,
The demons tell him no one will care,
He hides his arms, the scars and cuts,
He only wishes he had the guts,
His skin the canvas, the razor his brush,
He loves to sit and watch the blood gush,
He hates himself and his demons inside,
The pain in his eye he cannot hide,
Around his head and through his soul,
His body and mind have taken the toll,
To get rid of the demons, kill the pain,
Put an end to the silly game,
No matter what, there will be a pain in his heart,
He will always be worlds apart,
From reality and the lies he was told,
He will never have the chance to grow old.

Grace Kemp (16)

TROUBLES

If our troubles were on paper
We would brush away the ink,
Just like a small child,
We tell ourselves not to think
Of the problems that surfaced today,
Just let our minds wander,
Let our minds stray,
Think of the friend you can't wait to meet,
Whether you're young, delicate and sweet,
Or whether you're older trying to make ends meet,
Don't let your troubles take over your life
If you sort them out fast they cause less of a fight.

Shannon Jackson (13)

PRESSURE

Looking at my Instagram
I have to check my Twitter
Update my Facebook status
Check all my other networks
Just before my dinner.

I think my boyfriend's cheating
I think I like that guy
My best friends have ditched me
And I think I want to cry.

All the girls bully me
Due to the face I watch MLP
I wish I could fit in
And go through this stage
With friends that have my back.

Spots appearing on my face
It looks like pepperoni pizza
I want to dress oh-so-pretty
And have a party round my place.

Amy Ashcroft
Fareham Academy, Fareham

THE DEAR OLD MAN OF VICTORIA ROAD

The dear old man of Victoria Road,
'Ninety years young!' he said.
With his old rocking chair
And cheeky young glare,
He sat on his porch and sang . . .

'Young children of now, small child of today,
Put your phone away, away, away!'
And the children laughed,
Threw rocks at the man
And shouted, 'Ha, ha, okay!'

But one small child in his gang of friends,
Felt sorry for the man and stayed.
'Are you okay?'
He whispered in slight
And rocked the old man to sleep.

Years flew by and time went on,
The boy grew up,
The man grew old,
But their friendship sparked a hearty goodbye,
When the man died ninety-nine young.

More years passed, the house was lost,
The rocking chair creaked in the wind.
A father and son stepped into the house,
The father smiled at his kin.

'Do you know why we're here?' he asked.
'No, but it's way too cold.'
'Did you know, young Haymisch Greene,
You were named after the dear old man of Victoria Road?'

Amber Greep (14)
Hele's School, Plympton

THE ATTENTIVE ARTIST

If I had to paint your eyes,
I would have to mix the blue of the sky,
With the green of the sea
And the gold of unmined lands.

If I had to paint your hair,
I would double check it was the right length,
That it tickled your shoulders,
A dusting of cinnamon.

If I had to paint your hands,
I would need boxes of paper for
The long, elegant fingers
And the pale ivory skin.

If I had to paint your arms,
They would be free of bracelets and trinkets,
With scatters of freckles, here and there,
Like leaves falling in May.

If I had to paint your lips,
I would do it carefully and precisely,
Making sure I had caught the subtle curves and lines,
The soft red between ruby, garnet and jasper.

And, if I had to paint your lips,
I would paint them with mine on top.

Nancy Collis (13)
Hele's School, Plympton

THE BLINDED TRUTH

Those people who work for the unknown he
Do they know how to love or even dream?
If you stared into their soul all you would see,
Is a silver chain locked never to be free.

Their hearts of ice and their eyes like coal,
Trampling on content spirits,
Every life is already sold.
Never have they known such word of human rights,
All they have been told is to never look back only fight.

The desert watches as the children cry,
Hope and tranquillity are now known as a lie.
As our backs are turned from this way of living,
We are left only hearing stories
Our eyes left blind to seeing.

Whilst you sit back and watch the gentle clouds pass by,
Think about the twisted tear
Of which the Earth children have once cried.
For as your kin lay still sleeping safely, silently, softly in bed,
Another child lay on the dancing sand . . . dead.

Savannah Shepherd (13)

Hele's School, Plympton

THINK

Why bully? You make them feel small,
If you get angry go get a stress ball.
Cyber bullying or face to face,
Don't mess around it's not chase the ace.
Think of what you're doing, before you do it,
What if it was you, what if you were hit?
Think of all the pain, you made that person scared,
You could get in trouble, so what's the point there?
The victim is so worried but they need to get it out,
And then they think if they do that they'll have a lot of doubts.
Please don't bully, it's not a cool thing,
You think you're awesome 'cause you wear bling.
Anything is better than bullying!

Rebecca Bracher (13)
Hele's School, Plympton

ROSIE

Abandoned school, in this abandoned classroom . . .
In the darkness.
Not once was this place gloomy,
Covered in tiles, that alternate narrow hole.

I met Rosie; she's different.
Something I've never established in my life,
I placed my warm hands onto my ravishing Rosie.

Louisa Luff (13) & Eleanor Wollwebber (13)
The Thomas Aveling School, Rochester

MEDUSA

A dismal person standing here,
With black walls and school desks; pushed back like
Sugar running through a sieve.
As I carried on walking, on the wrong side of town;
Here I was the rundown, but everything has changed.
In a blink of an eye,
The noise of tumbleweed, running through
A servant's room, in the great palace.

They don't care if we breathe!
My heart turned into yesterday's nightmare.

Logan Haddrell & Benjamin Small
The Thomas Aveling School, Rochester

CHAINED

When I wake, I hear the wind whirling above,
With a peep hole for a window, covered by a black cord.
But surprisingly, a single comment or speech, about the great upper deck,
Chink . . . chink . . . chink . . .
The chains were in the police-force.

I peered anxiously at a black hole that sucked the life out,
Whizzing cars passed but finally it did,
Died in a car crash,
Like that!

They can crawl under your skin, and make you feel like the slaves!

Emily Watson & Toby Carlyon
The Thomas Aveling School, Rochester

SHE HEARS A QUIET THUD

She hears a quiet thud;
From the clip-clop of men, and their shoes, as they pass by;
Off in the distance.
I closed my eyes and dreamt about how many men?
How many men would be all over me?
But they did so much for their country!
Broken parts;
Shattered to the ground.
Breaking the ice, revealing the bed of grass beneath;
They were all envious of how beautiful it looked!

Callum Heard & Flynn Hope
The Thomas Aveling School, Rochester

UNTITLED

My name is Elena, I live in Egypt,
I had no choice but to pick up the useless situation;
As I walked just like a builder in a rundown place,
I learnt all the tips and tricks not even sparing a penny; for me,
I know the blossom tree, that held thousands of wishes,
Which pointed to the sky.

Pavan Badesha & Leonie Walcock
The Thomas Aveling School, Rochester

UNTITLED

I belong here, I do,
I know I do,
I belong in this and no one cares.

She is alone.
Young female, mature failure.

All my life, I've been beautiful,
Everyone loved me,
I then walked closer,
I could see her outfit,
She was worn down.

That back there,
That depressing piece,
Echoes followed by another,
It had seemed forever until it opened,
A doubt,
A jealousy,
Caused by a Greek God,
I was wrong, all along.

Ahmed Sultan (13) & Sam Bennison (13)
The Thomas Aveling School, Rochester

YOUNG WRITERS INFORMATION

We hope you have enjoyed reading this book - and that you will continue to enjoy it in the coming years.

If you like reading and writing poetry drop us a line, or give us a call, and we'll send you a free information pack.

Alternatively if you would like to order further copies of this book or any of our other titles, then please give us a call or log onto our website at **www.youngwriters.co.uk**

Young Writers Information
Remus House
Coltsfoot Drive
Peterborough
PE2 9BF
(01733) 890066